Humorous Hunting Tales
from
New Brunswick

by

Ray Dillon

Illustrated by

Chas Goguen

Neptune Publishing Company Ltd.
Saint John • New Brunswick • Canada

A paperback original from Neptune Publishing Company Ltd.
10 9 8 7 6 5 4 3

The publisher wishes to acknowledge and thank the Department of the New Brunswick Culture and Sports Secretariat for their assistance in this publication.

Canadian Cataloguing In Publication Data

Dillon, Ray - 1951-

Grin and Bear it!: New Brunswick: New Brunswick humorous hunting stories/by Ray Dillon.

ISBN: 1-896270-43-3
      1. Hunting--New Brunswick--Humour. I. Title.

  SK35.G74 2006   799.209715'1   C2006-901944-4

Editor: Susan Webber
Typesetter: Chas Goguen
Illustrator: Chas Goguen
Cover Design: Paul Evans

Printed and bound in Canada

Neptune Publishing Company Ltd.
PO Box 6941, Station A, Saint John, New Brunswick, E2L 4S4

Karrie & Gary

"Just would
like to say
thank you
very much"

Dedication

**This book is dedicated to my wife Doreen,
to my mother Mary
and to my late father Andrew.**

Phyllis

maureen

and me

June 2008

ACKNOWLEDGEMENTS

There are many people who are at least partly responsible for bringing this book from the inner recesses of my mind to the printed page. First, I must thank my loving wife Doreen who has served not only as my soul mate for the past thirty-five years but also as one of my biggest fans and supporters. She has witnessed some of the hilarious antics of some of our hunters, both at the table where she has served up fantastic home cooked meals and at our lodge after an exciting adventure. She has consistently encouraged me to write of these forays into the realm of real life bordering on fiction and has stood beside me from day one.

Another stalwart supporter who has encouraged me to pursue my writing, a pastime I love passionately, is Sue Rickards. Sue, who is well known in rural New Brunswick for a heart as big as the St. John River valley and for helping so many kids and adults realize their potential and their dreams has been the "wind beneath my wings". You will always hold a special place in my heart, Sue.

I must always remember to be grateful for my dear, kindly father, Andrew William Dillon Sr., deceased now many years, who introduced me to hunting as a young child. Dad taught me to enjoy the outdoors and the hunt but also instilled the ethics and sincerity that such a sport demands. I was a mere boy but he showed me how to become a man. As well, I wish to thank my mother, Mary Dillon for so many things too numerous to mention. She raised four boys in hard times and kept us on the straight and narrow… at least most of the time.

I have to thank my big brother Jim who helped me bag my first ruffed grouse in a round about way and younger brothers, Ken and Andrew who helped mould me into someone who could see the humorous side of just about anything that the good Lord sent our way. Jim especially has always been there to encourage and support me and has inspired me to write my memoirs about growing up to succeed despite being Irish proud but dirt poor.

Finally, I must admit there are too many friends and acquaintances and hunters who have either offered encouragement about my book or who supplied the adventures I had to include in it. May you all be blessed and "May you all be an hour in Heaven before the devil knows you're dead!"

Ray P. Dillon
Keswick Ridge, NB March 20, 2006

FOREWORD

As I sat in the warm glow of firelight, watching the snow swirl down outside our dining hall windows, my mind wandered back to the first time I ever encountered the hunting phenomenon. It was a crisp autumn morning in October and I was dragging behind as my dad and older brother Jim walked along an old logging road on a hardwood ridge. Our destination was a woodlot we were cutting on Crown land. We needed fourteen cord of wood per winter to heat our old farmhouse and Dad purchased the right to cut hardwood or "stumpage" on that ground so we were packing double in bladed axes and a bucksaw for the job.

Dad was a hard worker and always had the foresight not to miss an opportunity for food for our table so he also carried an old single shot H&R 12 gauge shotgun. I was walking behind Dad and Jim and watching my feet hit the ground when Dad whispered with anticipation, "Hold it boys. There's a bird." Instantly, I raised my head and looked in the direction Dad was aiming the shotgun. It was magnificent. It was a big male "drummer" grouse strutting along the ground, hopping up on an old fallen log. He just started to drum (beat his wings rapidly, trapping air under them and making a drumming sound) when Dad brought him down in a hail of birdshot and floating feathers. The acrid smell of gun powder mingled with the sweet smell of mountain ferns and damp earth and the sun shone down. The ridge was ablaze in yellows and scarlet and orange leaves and I scurried over and latched onto that bird much like a cat would a mouse. The bonus came that evening with the tender meat cooked in butter and salt and pepper that evening. It was delicious and I was excited and proud to have been part of putting it on our humble table.

I was hooked on hunting from that day forward.

In 1983, I worked as a provincial Park Warden at Mactaquac Provincial Park. I loved meeting people and worked with other Park Wardens who quickly realized that hunting was one of my greatest passions in life. One Park Warden asked me if I'd like to write down some of my hunting stories for an outdoor magazine his friends were putting together. That was the beginning of a career in writing that has led me to write outdoor columns for ten plus years for the *Telegraph Journal*, the *Daily Gleaner* and the *Oromocto Post* and a dozen outdoor magazines in the United States and Canada. I am currently a member of the Outdoor Writers Association of America and the New England Outdoor Writers Association and contribute monthly articles to several magazines.

In the fall of 1989, I started guiding hunters for moose, black bear, white tailed deer, ruffed grouse, woodcock and fishers for trout and Atlantic salmon. It was from these hunting and fishing expeditions that I gleaned the material for this book. At times, these antics and adventures have been almost unbelievable and I am sure, had I not experienced them first hand, I would have had difficulty in accepting them as factual. They have always been enjoyable adventures and oft times, hilarious so it is my hope that you will enjoy reading them as much as I have enjoyed reliving them as I put pen to paper. Incredible as it may seem, such hunters and guides do venture into the pristine beauty of New Brunswick's wilderness. Even more incredible is the obvious fact that they actually find their way back out of those woods after bringing fantastic tales to tell. So now folks, please curl up in your favorite chair by a crackling fire and enjoy my book. Be forever thankful that laughter is indeed the best medicine we can take and we should take it daily in huge doses.

TABLE OF CONTENTS

Chapter 1
A Saint... I Ain't!

To enhance your appreciation of what I am about to divulge, perhaps we should start with a bit of an autobiography! I was born in rural New Brunswick, a 1951 model, auburn haired, pureblood Irishman who grew through a troubled childhood into a troubled adulthood. My dear grey-haired, old Mama had delivered four boys by middle age, spaced four years apart. Any hopes my Dad may have had for creating a baseball team must have been dashed after that sixteen year period.

I was second in line to the throne with one older brother, Jim who used his superior age and strength to regularly beat the potatoes out of me on the slightest of excuses. My Mama, known throughout our small farming community as a dear, sweet woman who was a good and faithful friend and neighbour, was a holy terror when it came to raising four young ruffians. She'd take a switch or "gad" as she called it, made from the supple Hazel-nut bush, and proceed to administer corrective instruction to Jim and me. The other brothers came along later in life when Ma had mellowed somewhat and so daily "beatings" or "switchings" were no longer used to teach the straight and narrow.

As I look back on my life, I am somewhat surprised that I survived and although I am Protestant, I firmly believe that Ma came from a Catholic background where exorcisms were routinely carried out. I know she often loudly proclaimed that she'd "beat the devil out of me or die trying!" She must have succeeded since she's still alive, in her eighties and nasty as ever and I have no horns or glowing red eyes, at least not through the work week!

I could tell you about all the nasty, naughty things I did as a young boy, about locking my friend from next door in our hay mow and then tearing down one of those big black hornet nests. I could go on and tell about walking calmly outside to listen to my friend beg, cuss and to see him come rushing out of the mow window some twelve feet up, flaying at the swarm of hornets all wanting a piece of him. I could tell you of a young man who watched *Batman* on a new television set and promptly made cardboard wings to run and jump headfirst off our woodshed… darned things didn't work! I could also tell you about how I terrorized the neighbourhood but I won't!

Instead, I want to share with you how a young, red-headed, Irishman used to sneak out the open window in one room of a two room school while the new school teacher snoozed, just to run through the patch of woods behind the school, how I became passionate about hunting at the ripe old age of five and fishing the year before. Anything and everything that pertained to the outdoors interested me; fascinated my young mind.

I loved all animals with a passion that burned deep within my soul and guiding hunters and fishers just seemed to come naturally to me. My first guiding experience came when I was nine. My younger cousin, a seven year old, had become intrigued by my fishing tales so he begged me to take him and teach him to fish. In a heartbeat, plans were laid for early the next Saturday morning and just an hour after sunrise, I was leading my cousin through some heavy cedar swamp to a stream we called the Millbrook. It seems so funny today when I hunt my way past this huge brook where fat trout used to lie in shaded pools, a brook I can now almost straddle! Of course back then, six inch trout were big trout and walking a mile or so on the back woodlots was pure wilderness to us kids!

I can still recall showing Andrew how to bait the hook and jerk on it when the fish nibbled but the funniest part of that memory came at lunchtime. My cousin was in awe of me and expressed it in so many flattering words. I had caught several nice trout to his one and now, with the aid of a Zippo lighter my parents didn't know I had, I set about building a campfire. I fashioned a toaster from a hardwood switch, taking particular pleasure in thinking that this was one switch Ma wouldn't be using on me! "Hurry up, Ray, I'm some hungry!" I must leave out the verbal expletives that were typical of my cousin and so many other young men in our farming community. Yep, bilingual they were… broken English and perfect profanity!

I set about as any good guide would, showing Andrew how to clean the fish and my intentions were honourable... at least up to this point. Then old Satan set in and when Andrew held up a half cleaned trout and asked if this was okay, I smiled and said "yeah!" I then took the fish with most of its insides still in place, pushed it on the toaster stick and held it over the crackling fire. Within a couple of minutes, the smell of fish cooking wafted over the area. The skin was hardly blackened and crisp when Andrew became insistent that it must be ready to eat. "Yep, you grab this one," I grinned. As long as I live, I don't believe I will ever see a more honest look of revulsion on anyone's face, nor will I ever hear the great oaths and cuss words that spewed with raw fish and fish guts from the mouth of one so young! I laughed so hard that I fell off the log I was sitting on and the woods rang out with the nasty awful names my cousin called me! Well deserved I might add. Ahh... my first guiding experience!

As I grew up on our small farm, I was required to do chores such as "slopping" (feeding) the hogs, feeding the chickens and milking the cows. Jim and I divided up the workload so each of us would have time to fish and hunt but both of us hated to do the milking. Morning came early to farm boys and we had no time to dally! We had to do chores in our school clothes and by the time all was done, we'd step onto the school bus smelling like a Jersey or a Holstein cow. The local girls would turn up their pretty noses as we'd walk by and usually, guys would readily save us an empty seat where we could sit without touching them. The guys had learned early on that you might think an Irishman smells like a cow but you don't tell him to his face!

I bagged my first Ruffed Grouse when I was eleven after arguing with Jim over what I thought was a stump. "No Ray, dummy, that's not a stump, it's a "partridge"; a local term for Ruffed Grouse.

4

At that moment, in the lengthening shadows of a cool October afternoon, the boy became a hunter. The stump started displaying and I drew a bead. Dad's old Harrington and Richardson single shot twelve gauge shotgun spat fire and number six birdshot. It kicked viciously bruising my shoulder but it sure whacked that bird too!

In a flash, I was bounding over brush and stumps to gather up the still fluttering "drummer" grouse. Its wings flailed wildly and its sharp clawed feet squirmed but I held firm! Later on that evening, Dad commented on just how good that grouse tasted, all sautéed in butter and although I enjoyed it immensely myself, the gratification of the accomplishment was savoured much more!

By the ripe old age of twelve, I was sneaking out of my bedroom window evenings with Dad's shotgun, crossing the kitchen roof and climbing down the ladder to hunt back of our farm. Ma would not approve I knew, so I was forced to do it surreptitiously, leaving bagged birds on the chopping block by our woodshed for my Dad to find and clean. This went on for most of that fall bird season until Dad approached Jim one evening to clean his own birds when he bagged them. Jim denied even getting the birds and the following evening, when I had dropped off six fat grouse and sneaked back through my bedroom window, Ma and Pa sat calmly on my bed staring at me. Ma, the dominant parent in our family, was the first to scream at me.

"What are you doing with Dad's gun?" That question I felt was rhetorical since she knew darned well why I had his gun! "Don't you know, you are too young to hunt… even get a license? What if you shot somebody? You'd end up in prison!" Ma had that "I'm gonna beat the devil out of you" look in her one good eye. Mama had one good eye, and one glass eye that drifted south on occasion. (That made her appear like she was looking at you and her feet at the same time and when people on the street saw her bad eye drooping and pointing at the ground, they'd stop to help her look for whatever she might have dropped!) Dad had sat silently, listening to Ma rave. Finally he stopped and cleared his throat.

"Now Ray, you know you aren't allowed to hunt without someone being with you. Still, we can use all those birds for winter." He looked at Ma who was gritting her false teeth, making mad dog sounds and glaring at me and the floor… all at the same time! "Well, you probably aren't doing any harm, so long as you are careful, and…" he stopped and thought for a moment. "You sure bagged a lot of birds this fall!" He stopped and looked at Ma who was now calming down and wiping the foam from the corners of her mouth. "If he can hunt deer like he hunts birds Ma… maybe we should teach him how to use the rifle!" After that, it sure felt good to strut down stairs with Dad's gun, slip into my red plaid wool mackinaw and yell "see ya later."

During my high school years, I hunted with tunes from Elvis, Herman's Hermits and the Beatles replaying in my head. My interest in the mechanics of fishing and hunting had become keen and it was no longer enough to see the fish or birds or deer that I pursued. Although I enjoyed fishing, hunting became an obsession with me, especially chasing the elusive whitetail. I began studying the animal. I read any and all literature I could find about deer and hunting them and I sifted through tons of information. I examined scrapes and scats and rubs and deer carcasses whenever I had the opportunity. I finally began to draw my own conclusions about these animals.

For example, I found that some bucks rub the same trees over and over again, every autumn… unless they were shot the previous year (the deer, not the tree). A spike horn is not always a spike horn unless he only grows spikes all his life… in which case he really is a spike horn! I found that you might need to wait ten minutes or so before going after a deer you have shot… but <u>only if he has run off</u>!

As my teen years passed into history, the world changed. I graduated from high school with a degree in FHJ (Fishing/Hunting/Jigging class) and stopped using drugs. Please let me clarify this for you. No, I was not a pothead although my head is shaped sort of funny. The strongest drug I ever used was alcohol and mostly in the form of beer or wine, good wine… you know, good tasting stuff, the kind that comes with a screw on cap… ahh… quality Vino! No, truthfully, my heaviest drug was Tylenol and then only when I had a head or tooth ache. Once out of school, my headaches and tooth aches disappeared and I never had a sick day, something that led my home room teacher to suspect I had been faking all those years! I was insulted! Well, I quit the "drugs" anyhow!

I got married and went out into the world to work but I still spent every minute I could in the woods. It was several years into our marriage before my wife… she's a blonde… began to suspect that weekend drives on old woods roads were more than nature drives. She would also ask why I needed to go to the woods and sit up in a tree stand all autumn long, just to think. I told her it was because of a nervous condition with the medical name, "Iwannabucknow!" My poor wife never did figure that one out! And so life continues with this now OLD Irishman living his life in the wilds of New Brunswick, hunting and fishing and guiding any and all who want to partake of the sport of kings and queens and the occasional fairy! My darling wife cooks for our hunters and fishers and puzzles over life's little questions like "Why don't we "catch" a buck or why don't we call a bunch of bruins a flock and why isn't rutting season called the "want to have sex" season?" I hope you enjoy the antics of our hunters as you read on…, the joys, the successes, the dismal failures and those things almost too fantastic to believe! A wise man once stated "It's not the trophy hanging on the wall, but just how he got to be there that makes so many great memories! The sport of hunting is to be enjoyed long after the actual event has transpired!" Well… I must confess…, that wise man is me and I did say that!

Chapter 2
The Missed Adventures of Hawkeye & Me!

When I decided to start up an outfitting business, I felt quite comfortable in offering guided hunts for Ruffed Grouse and Wood-cock, and for White Tailed Deer. After all, I had commenced hunting at an early age and continued to study and chase Ruffed Grouse and deer through my adolescent and troubled teen years. Black Bear hunting was a horse or hunt of a different color!

The only bear experience I had came in bits and pieces and while I knew a reasonable amount about bears, I had never studied nor hunted them. If I intended to offer guided hunts for the critters, I knew what I had to do.

A friend of mine we'll call him Hawkeye for reasons you will discover later on, wanted to guide for me. A friendly, good natured man, Hawkeye's talents with a rifle left much to be desired. When he first hunted with me, they may have been influenced by his fear of bears! "I don't have a problem with bears," he confided in me one evening as he followed me to a bait site. We were baiting late and I was a bit apprehensive about baiting in the evening. I stopped to tie a bootlace and old Hawkeye passed me and pushed down the brushy "clear cut" path into the mature woods. It was a hot evening in late September and I remember so vividly the sweat oozing down the hollow of my back, my shirt clinging to my body, the heavy humid air, the steady hum of biting insects and the crash… thud, thud of running feet! Hmmmmm. Hawkeye rushed by me like a runaway freight train, eyes bulging, mouth wide open, and a look of sheer terror on his face. "Hey, what's wrong, Hawkeye?"

"Run Ray, run like hell… bear… big bear," he called back over his shoulder. I stood and watched him leap over fallen logs and debris in that clear cut in a manner that would have made a big buck deer proud! Man, he could move when he wanted to! And he was still carrying the bag with the bait in it.

I could hear a commotion in the woods behind me so I turned to face an obviously angry bear, popping its teeth, shaking its head and slavering. Ears laid flat back and little reddish pig eyes told me it was time to depart this area but what was the bear so angry about. Hawkeye, some hundred and twenty yards away and still running yelled back once again "Run Ray, she's got a cub!" Okay! Enough said! I backed off, still facing her. I walked backward slowly… back towards the truck, a quarter mile distant, where Hawkeye stood with the truck door open and yelling for me to come. I giggled nervously as I approached him.

"Thanks for leaving me behind, buddy!" He stared at me, his eyes still bulging. He still clutched the bag of bait. "And why didn't you drop that bag of bait when she came out of the woods?" He grinned, "I ain't that stupid. That bait is for the bait bucket, not her! She's damned lucky I didn't have my rifle. Why I would have stood my ground. I ain't afraid of no bears. If she had got my "dander" up (a local reference to temperament), I'd a grabbed her single handed!" The big sow showing up right at the truck, busting from the woods and posturing, ferociously charging the truck and us, interrupted his obvious sudden bravado. We got in and closed the doors and Hawkeye fired up the engine and hurriedly drove away. I was also startled by her aggressive behavior but I had to laugh as Hawkeye bounced us recklessly along the old logging road, peering in the rearview mirror as we went.

Hawkeye wanted to conquer his fear of bears and after that incident with the nasty sow, he had a hate on for the critters. He came to me one evening with the idea of me guiding him so he could bag a black bear. Of course I would have to be right there with him. "Okay, I will. I need the experience anyhow and I'll start baiting for the spring hunt." Spring hunt, fall hunt, even if it had been a year round hunt, I knew very little about the process of baiting and hunting bruins and to demonstrate to you just how little I knew, it was my belief that we had few black bears in the province. After all, I spent a heck of a lot of time in our woods and had seen only a half a dozen bears ever! Hawkeye knew even less about those black ghosts.

"Yes sirree… boy! Ya gotta fetch them critters with the rottenest old maggot filled, stinky smellin' meat ya kin find. Take it and put it in the deepest, darkest swamp ya kin find, a good twenty miles back in the woods and ya do it agin twenty miles or more away, an' ya keep doin' it in every swamp hole till ya got as many baits as ya kin, maybe a hundred or so. Don't wear anything but rubber boots and don't handle any o' the trees or bushes an check them baits every week or two. You'll git "barrs" (known to most of civilized society as bears) in there, for sure!" The advice of the grizzled old outfitter/guide landed on me like water hitting a sponge and within days, I was busy driving out into the remotest country I could find. It took two hours of steady driving time and all my strength and endurance to wrestle the forty-five gallon steel drum half full of gut wrenching maggot filled liquefying slop into a bug filled black mud swamp. After two full days of repeat procedures, I had succeeded in creating four baits. It didn't really matter though that absolutely nothing hit them cause they were so far back in the woods, that we would have had to camp out there just to hunt them!

"There's got to be an easier way," I murmured as I sat eating a late lunch in the cool afternoon breezes on a hardwood ridge. Something black, stark black against the green canopy caught my eye, something moving towards me, lumbering, sniffing the air. I dropped my ham and cheese sandwich on the log where I reposed and backed off cautious and quietly, my eyes constantly on the big bear. He came to the log and gulped down my sandwich, licking the log where it had dropped. I moved off into the woods and out onto the logging road some fifty yards distant.

I was half way to my truck when the light bulb came on in my head and I found my self walking and muttering at the same time. "Why that bear is out here next to a well traveled logging road in the middle of the afternoon? He ain't down in that bloody swamp two miles over! Why? And he wouldn't touch that slop in the barrel for the past couple of weeks but he ate my sandwich like it was candy! Why that lyin' old bas(illegitimate son)!" So much for trusting the wisdom of another outfitter, that is, competitor!

Over the next few weeks, I began to debunk all the false information I had relied on and things started to come together! I really became radical experimenting with various baits, bait sites and methods of baiting. I found that contrary to what you may read in some magazines or books, bears don't care whether you are wearing rubber boots or going bare foot. You don't need to use heavy steel barrels for baits… unless of course you have a fetish for wrestling such items way back in the woods and speaking of that, you don't need to bait way back in the woods! There are bears in many places including right next door to you if you live in a rural area. You may have never seen many bears but start baiting and using good foods for bait, breads, fresh meats and bones, candies and sweets

(NO CHOCOLATE) and you'll see bears… lots of them coming from the same woods you thought were empty!

Well, I finally had lots of bears coming to my baits, baits easily accessible, some right along side of old roads, on forest and field edges and in clear cuts, on hardwood ridges and in or near swamps. I called Hawkeye and told him to go and purchase his bear license. "We're ready to hunt!"

I met the old outfitter in the woods one afternoon as he traveled around baiting and I strolled to the back of his truck purposely. "Oh, I see you gave up on steel barrels and maggot filled slop. You are using good bait and five gallon buckets now, Charley." He felt uncomfortable but questioned what I was doing there. "Why, baiting here, Charley. You must have every distant swamp baited by now." He cleared his throat and informed me that he had three baits within a mile of where we now talked. "Oh, gave up on that old "swamp" every twenty miles or so, eh?" He drove off, a bit red faced and grimacing from the verbal exchange, not daring to suggest that I vacate these lands. His lies to a young naïve guide had come back to bite him… right on the posterior and it was appropriate!

Hawkeye brought his big 7 mm magnum, all scoped with a 3x12x40 mm duplex and his new 4x4 Ford into my yard the next afternoon. It was nearing three p.m. and a hot, sultry, muggy afternoon. Big dark storm clouds loomed on the horizon but we drove out to our first bait site anyhow. I had built a huge tree stand in four maples overlooking the bait site, and right next to the old logging road but we decided to watch the bait from the truck for a while. Those thunderheads were fast approaching and really looked ominous so we sat and talked in whispered tones and watched. This gave Hawkeye an opportunity to smoke, something he appreciated much more than I. He'd light up one of his extra long, King sized, whatever the heck they were and sit back in the seat to suck or drag on it. This was a thirty second process where his bloodshot eyes would bug out more than usual, his cheeks would actually cave inward and his tiny chicken chest would expand to almost normal size. Then he'd spend the next few seconds exhaling and coughing uncontrollably prompting me to make some wry comment about how good that crap must be.

Soon, the steady hum of biting insects attempting to enter the smoky cab of his truck was drowned out by vicious rumbling noises and the slight breeze dropped to dead calm. "Better roll up your window," I cautioned just as a heavy lightning bolt flashed by to split a tree in the clear cut with fire and flying wood shreds. A huge clap of thunder followed almost immediately and Hawkeye started the Lord's Prayer or maybe he was cursing… I don't know. At any rate, I never saw a manual roll-up window go up as fast as his did. At first it rained and then it hailed. The winds gusted viciously and chain lightning filled the sky. "Whew! Got every thing but a tornado," Hawkeye grinned. "Ain't you glad we ain't sittin' in that tree stand of yours right now?" "Yeh," I coughed. "Put out that damned cigarette before I suffocate or get lung cancer myself!" He complied.

The winds died down and the dark clouds moved south and the woods came alive once more with birds singing and of course, the hum of those insects hovering in cloud formation. It was still muggy and I wiped a trickle of sweat from my brow and glassed the cut with my powerful binoculars. Suddenly, we had bears, several bruins approaching our bait. Two yearlings with a big old sow showed up, as did a smaller sow with a tiny cub. She waited until the big sow and her juveniles had selected fresh tidbits and moved off twenty yards and then sent her youngster up a big yellow birch tree. She came in warily, watching the other bears and grabbed a large bone. Moving back to the birch and her cub, she lay down and held it between her paws, gnawing on it just as a dog would. Her cub joined her, trying to tear tidbits of meat from it at first and then attempting to get her to roll on her back so he could suckle. It was a pleasant scene, one we had never witnessed before but would do so, over and over in the future.

An hour passed and several other bears of various sizes came in. At one point, we had nine bruins scattered in the clearing but a sudden breeze brought them all to their feet and saw them scatter into the surrounding woods. We sat there in the truck cab in silent wonder. Why had they acted so? Our silent question was soon answered as a huge boar came waddling up the old road towards the bait and us. He had appeared at two hundred yards but was closing the distance steadily. "Holy sh…! My good Lord, it's big as a Volkswagen," I hissed. Hawkeye just sat there, breathing raggedly. The closer the bear came, the heavier Hawkeye breathed. "Put the gun on him, Hawk," I whispered. I too was fighting an adrenaline surge as I watched this magnificent bear! "Calm down and aim right high in the brisket or if he turns, take him in the front shoulder… but you need to calm down!" Hawkeye was like a man possessed. He raised his rifle and aimed out of the truck window. "No man, you got to get out of the truck! This ain't legal!" He looked over at me and shakily grasped the truck door handle, opening the door. The bear stopped and looked our way.

"Freeze, Hawk! The son of a gun is lookin' right at us! Wait till he starts walking again and then take him! Don't you miss!"

When I think back to that fateful first night, I partially blame my lack of bear guiding experience for what happened next. The bear started walking toward us once more and Hawkeye steadied his gun between the open door and the cab frame. Perhaps it was my

"don't you miss" that made him go to pieces or perhaps it was the incredible size of that bear… I don't know.

He looked over at me; his eyes still bugging out wildly and his chest heaving and jerked his head back to the scope. The bear was within fifty yards now and had stopped face on with head raised, sniffing the air. "KA-POW!" The shot rang through the green valley and a small flurry of dirt and debris next to the bear's right side indicated a miss, a clean miss, an incredible miss, an unbelievable miss! The bear should have turned inside out and crashed off into the surrounding vegetation. Instead, he reared up on his hind legs and sniffed the air. "KA-POW!" With that and the green leafy branch that toppled off to the bear's left side, he now felt that this wasn't the safest place to be. He charged off into the woods, crashing through or mowing down brush and small trees in his escape. Hawkeye was still breathing raggedly and staring wildly as I convinced him that the bear was gone and he should drop his gun and unload it. "Did I get him…? I had to… I must have got him… didn't I?" With a consoling look, I stared at him and stated matter of factly, "No, you missed him twice, but he might die laughing or catch a cold from the bullets! After all, you did bag a nice maple branch and you probably killed several ants who were innocent bystanders on the ground beside him!"

Several missed black bears later, I had resigned myself to quit guiding anyone who remotely resembled Hawkeye. I would give up hunting and become a vegetarian monk in some far off land where all I would do is sit on my backside and hum all the day long, my only care or concern being whether I hummed on key or not. Then, when the bear hunt looked darkest and Hawkeye was running low on ammunition, the bears started getting used to coming to our baits and being shot at. They seemed to lose all fear of being hit. I could see why, and one hot fly filled evening, he connected! My Lord! The bear was probably as surprised as Hawkeye and me but nonetheless, he bagged his first bruin and only after missing seven others!

Hawkeye guided for me during the tumultuous years as I was learning the business and whenever a client missed or screwed up on a bruin, he'd sit back, shake his head and recount the great bear hunt he had experienced and the one shot he used to take his bear! Yes sir, he was careful never to mention all the hunts he had shared with missed opportunities! When a hunter/client would ask why he had the nickname "Hawkeye", he'd shrug and lie like a rug. It was so far removed from the truth that no one would ever know, except maybe me, and I'll never tell… except maybe to tell you!

Chapter 3
The Bear and Harley Davidson

Here is a humorous story that happened to my son Terry and I one day. We were sitting on the sofa in our lodge, looking at pictures of bygone hunting and fishing days, discussing the upcoming bear hunting season and all of a sudden Terry says, "Sounds like a motorcycle driving up, Dad," as he shot an inquisitive glance towards the lodge windows. "Yeh, right! We're catering to Hell's Angels now," I grinned back. But there was no mistaking the deep guttural sounds of a Harley Davidson approaching although the subsequent "thud" that shook the lodge startled us. "Good Lord, what was that," I muttered loudly and headed for the front door. The sight that met my eyes brought both concern and wonder as I stared at the fellow picking himself up off the ground.

"Whew! What a rush!" His high-pitched nasal exclamation bespoke someone from the Cheech and Chong era of the seventies and his wardrobe screamed "BIKER!" Medium built with a good-sized potbelly, he had long, shoulder length, scraggly hair around the lower region of his head and top. His thick coke bottle glasses magnified his eyes to the size of an owl's. Those eyes had tiny pinpoint pupils caused by goodness knows what chemical or drug and his entire face, screened with a scruffy long beard held a deep red, almost purple hue as though he would explode at any moment. A black leather vest hung loosely over a "ban the bomb" t-shirt and faded, ragged blue jeans with cycle boots finished the look.

As he dusted himself off and righted his semi prone bike, he looked at us and grinned. "Whoa, sorry about that dudes! Didn't realize how far the hog would skid on grass. Guess I should a braked quicker! How's the bear thing lookin' man?" He strutted over to us and extended a grimy hand. "Harley's the name… just like my chopper… but don't let that fool ya. I'm a hunter, one hundred percent and I'm gonna get one big son of a gun of a bear, if I have to use my bare hands! Damn! My gun!"

Harley left Terry and I standing in the lodge doorway with open mouths and disbelief written all over our faces as he rushed over to his bike and the saddle scabbard that held his gun. He hurriedly unsheathed the weapon and peered through the scope. "Whew, she's okay dudes!" I grinned and interjected that we would visit the range and check his sights later. We helped Harley with his bags and gear, all strapped on the two-up-seat and backrest and soon he was roaming around the lodge, checking out pictures of hunters and their trophies and stroking our bear and deer mounts. As he patted a hundred and fifty pound live mount black bear, he rolled his eyes and shook his head as though he was having a seizure. "You okay, Harley?" "Yeh dude, I want one of these guys… right here!" "Well, hopefully you'll get one… only bigger," Terry smiled. Harley didn't respond. He just stood there hugging the bear… lost in his own fantasy.

We intended to have lunch and head out to finish baiting our bear areas so we invited Harley along. It proved to be an interesting ride. As we motored through the countryside, Harley scooted from one side of the van to the other staring out the windows like a schoolboy. "Holy sasquatch! You dudes got some big country up here in Canada! Crap! Look at the size of that rabbit! It's as big as a coyote back home! What a trip, man! What a trip!" Terry and I grinned at each other, both silently questioning what we had gotten ourselves into. At that point, we came to one of our bait areas and stopped. It was early afternoon in mid May, hot and sunny with accompanying flies that bite.

The flies quickly took a liking to Harley, judging by his fluency in profanity as we walked to the bait. A sudden woof, woof stopped us cold and a big sow bear with two cubs stood to face us. "Holy shit, dude! Bears! Real …*@#*@… bears! F… real bears! Let's get 'em dudes! Whoa! What a rush!" Despite the precariousness of our situation, Terry and I snickered and broke into uncontrollable laughter. The sow couldn't quite comprehend any of this and rushed off into the woods with her young ones in tow. Harley was jumping up and down and waving his arms, wide eyed and almost frothing at the mouth. Well, at least he was yelling and spitting! We finished baiting and headed for the last bait in the area. Harley was bouncing off the seats in the van, lunging back and forth and voicing loud profane expletives while spitting on my windows as he peered out. "The dudes in my bike club ain't gonna believe this," he screamed. Well, we certainly didn't and we were right here with him!

"Ya ain't gonna go too far away, are ya Ray?" Harley yelped while sitting on a twelve-foot high ladder tree stand some thirty yards off a clear cut and three miles from the main artery, a dirt topped logging road… in bear country. Although he had his 7 mm Magnum scoped rifle cradled in his arms, he had lost much of his hunting enthusiasm and all of his bravado by opening afternoon and had I been able to distinguish it beyond those huge magnified eyes, I'm fairly sure he was wide eyed in the throes of full blown terror. "I've got to bait a few baits but I'll be back, Harley, so don't worry. If a bruin shows up, just take careful aim and blister him, either high in the brisket or front shoulder. I've got to pick up one of my guides who wants to be back here tonight with me. See ya later!"

Harley watched me drive away from his perch in the big spruce tree, like a puppy dog pining for his master but as I glanced at the stand and the camouflaged hunter sitting on it, I was sure that he'd get over his anxiety soon after we left. The afternoon became evening all too soon and as my guide, Wayne and I drove down the country road to check on Harley, a strange sight met our eyes. Long beard and hair blowing behind him, a semi clad hunter came sprinting toward us. Suspenders drooping and pants sagging and red woolen underwear torn open at the chest, he charged along. We could see that the hunter was soaked in sweat as he neared the van and those thick spectacles were heavily fogged. I stopped the van and he thudded into the side of it, grasping for the door handle.

To see a man in such utter disarray and panic sent a chill down my spine. I cast a questioning glance at Wayne who was feeling the same chill. "Harley, are you okay? What happened? Why are you way out here?" He leaned half way in on the van floor, sucking in big gulps of warm evening air and then, with both Wayne and I firing rapid, concerned questions at him, he reached up into the shoulder of his underwear top and hauled out a pack of cigarettes, lighting one and inhaling deeply. After the ensuing coughing spell that must have lasted two minutes or more, the red faced Harley shook his head and squealed "Whew! What a rush!" Wayne and I were not reassured. He was three miles from his stand, semi dressed with no gun in sight and obviously in some mental shock or state of mind. Had he shot someone? What would possess a bear hunter to undertake such a journey, obviously at full speed ahead and leave his gun behind?

"Bear, great big f…@*#@#* bear! I got him, though, twice! Whew! What a rush!" Harley was waving his hands and gesturing

like a mad man and those owl eyes were so wide, you could count the blood vessels in them, under those magnifying glass lenses! I still wanted to question him, to assure both Wayne and I that all was well but he was raving so I packed him in for the ten minute ride to his stand. That ride took twenty-five minutes as we stopped along the way to gather up items of clothing he had shed as he fled the scene. We learned that a bear had indeed ventured out to the bait around eight o'clock and he had fired at it. The bear had fallen, stood back up, looked around and attempted to take food from the bucket. Harley fired once more and the bear walked back into the woods, glancing over his shoulder as he went. "Doesn't sound like it's hurt, Harley," I shook my head. "Oh yeh, dude! That son of a …censored… is mine! I nailed him twice. Then, I threw my rifle into the bushes, jumped to the ground, kind of turned my ankle, and I took off on the run. Sore ankle or not, I wasn't gonna stay around where no wounded bear was!"

His story told it all and both Wayne and I grinned as we listened. 'Why didn't you hold onto your gun and do like I instructed you? Remember Harley? Unload the gun, climb down and walk out to the logging road… not throw the gun, jump out of a twelve foot high ladder stand and run to the main road! Good lord, man! You could have been injured!" He shook his head. "I just wanted to be elsewhere," came his reply. We finally arrived at the bait site and walked to the stand. It took us several minutes to find his rifle lying in the dirt amidst a fir thicket but it didn't take us long to see what had really happened to our fearless bear hunter. Several minutes combing the site and the woods behind the bait turned up absolutely no blood or hair. Wayne wanted to push deeper into the woods but I told him that it would be senseless. We had probably an hour of daylight left so I suggested that we search the immediate area. "Look for bullet holes in the ground and trees," I instructed. "I really don't think Harley hit that bear, especially given the "slip" mark in the mud by the bait. I think he just startled the animal and it slipped and fell." Wayne circled the immediate area while I examined the vegetation directly behind the bait and in what I believed to be Harley's line of fire. Harley valiantly volunteered to stay at the van on the old logging road… in case we got lost, and needed him to honk the van horn.

Sure enough! The large rock maple tree that had stood for seventy years or more in this piece of real estate had fallen victim to Harley's 7 mm Magnum. The first bullet had sliced the ground in front of the tree, splashing grit onto the bear's belly, causing him to buck and slip. It had glanced off a small stone and embedded itself in the tree trunk at an upward angle at six inches from the ground. The second bullet had carried straight into the tree at six feet from ground level. I called Wayne over and showed him but Harley refused to come into the woods. I explained what we had found and added some good-natured ribbing. "Harley, I can see you thinking that first shot downed him, cause he did slip and fall, but what did you think when he stood up and started to feed? And what was that second shot all about? We have never seen a bear that stands six feet tall on all four, not even a grizzly!" Harley grinned sheepishly and mumbled that he was sure he had bagged his bear. "We could get the saw and cut that sucker down for you since you made two good shots on the maple. You could take that back home," I grinned. Harley was less than amused.

The following afternoon saw Harley back on his stand with both Wayne and I assuring him that most bears won't hurt you. "We'll stay nearby all evening," I promised, "but we need to do the other baits first. You'll be okay! Yes, that 7 mm Mag. is all the bear gun you need but you have to hit him where it hurts… forward shoulder or high in the brisket! Remember, sit quiet and stay there, after you shoot… and keep a hold of that rifle, Harley, okay?" Harley cast sullen looks in our direction as we walked to the van and drove off, almost as though he was blaming us for making him hunt the animal. "I can't believe that anyone would actually pay an outfitter to hunt something he's terrified of, can you," I asked Wayne. "Beats the hell out of me," he shrugged, "but that man is scared of bears… big time!"

We hurried and got done baiting fairly early and were sitting just up the road off the bait site at half past six. The evening held a slight breeze that scattered the swarms of flies and helped cool the warm May temperatures. "You suppose Harley will see anything there tonight, Ray," Wayne queried. I shrugged. "I don't know. If he sits quiet, maybe. I know we tracked it up good in there last night looking for the bear he missed but I scented it up good this afternoon when I put him out so we'll see. There are a good number of bears tending this bait." Ka-Pow! Ka-Pow! Ka-Pow! The roar of the rifle startled both of us and interrupted my conversation with Wayne but that didn't matter. As per our previous arrangement with the hunter, we waited for him to come to the road. Time passed, minutes and then almost an hour but no hunter came. "Ya think we should go in on him," Wayne whispered.

"No, sit tight. If he got something, he'll be out. If not, we'll go get him at dark."

Twenty minutes to dark, we heard two more loud shots and once again, we waited but Harley stayed put. At dark, we walked in to his stand and there he sat, trembling in his stand. "God, guys! I shot at two big bears. Did you hear me? One was an hour or more ago and the other less than a half hour ago, but I think I missed them both." To be sure, we checked the area with our flashlights but no blood or hair, or evidence of a hurried or sick bear could be found.

As we drove homeward, an obviously super charged Harley ranted in the rear seat, bouncing back and forth like he was on speed or something. Apparently the first bear he missed was a big white "v" (marking on chest), which is a bit uncommon to see. The second animal was the one that I grieved over, a beautiful cinnamon boar had come to the bait and was given a "Harley one gun salute" instead of the customary three gun salute, so it had made a hasty and unmarked departure.

By week's end, Harley had missed a total of seven New Brunswick black bears. "Gotta get a new scope," he grinned as he shook hands the morning of his departure. It was raining hard and I had attempted to persuade him to wait out the rain. "Hell no, dude! My hog has seen wet roads before... and you don't have to worry about bugs in your teeth in the rain!" He mounted his Harley Davidson and kicked the engine into that deep throaty roar that only a Harley can make. "Whew! What a rush, dudes! Bear hunting! I'll be back," came that high nasal yell. We stood in the doorway of our lodge and wondered how they'd ever let such a critter back into his own country. For that matter, how'd they ever let him come into ours?

Chapter 4
Dickie's Deer Hunt
or Psycho Man - Lost

I sat on the cabin steps and watched as a slick new van tooled down the drive. It had no plate on the front of it, often typical of vehicles from the USA, but the three guys inside left no question that they were hunters or at least had the urge to become hunters. Snow flakes were falling as these three heavily camouflaged guys disembarked, shivering in obviously new hunting clothes.

"Brrr, it's damned cold up heh in Canada! This place is paht of Canada, ain't it?"

I stood surveying the group, noticing new boots, new pants and hunting jackets that looked nice but rustled each and every time the lads breathed. "Yep, you're in the great white north… or at least it will be white come morning," I grinned. "You lads are from New England I'd say, so you must be… Dickie?" The geographically challenged spokesman, a diminutive little fellow, stepped forward and offered a tiny hand. He had the mighty grip of a… chicken, maybe not as strong, and I couldn't help but notice the one left eye that veered off viciously to the left while the other stared straight at me. The effect was unnerving since it started me thinking that he had summoned a thug to thrash me for secretly grinning at his size, and that darned left eye was looking for the brute to come around the corner any second!

Dickie wasn't what you'd call a handsome little man. He had

a half inch gap between two large front teeth, a heavy growth of chin whisker that came to a point below two thin lips and a pair of ears that… well, let's say they could come in handy for listening. He kind of reminded me of Dopey, one of the seven dwarfs. Now, Dickie's hunting companions weren't much of an improvement. After examining them visually, I sort of thought I'd be hearin' "duellin banjos" cause I'd swear they were right out of the movie *Deliverance*! One was Big Bob, aptly named. Long and lanky with stooped shoulders and hands that hung below his knees, Bob had the market cornered on stupid looks! A slack jaw that sported a square dimpled chin, eyes sunken into sallow cheek bones and a totally square forehead, he looked so out of place with the dwarf… I mean Dickie and the other guy. John, the final member of the group, had a medicine ball gut that threatened to drag both his new camo pants and jacket to the earth. Bulbous eyes, a round full, fat face, double… maybe triple chin and a shock of jet black hair that looked like straw thatch protruding from his camo hat, he looked like anything but a hunter. He was average in height but walked in a sort of squatted position and his bow- legged cant reminded me of someone attempting to carry a huge boulder, cradled low in his arms.

I helped the three unpack their gear, all new stuff with price tags still hanging on it. That small operation caused all three to puff and pant and sweat and prompted my questions. "You guys have hunted before… right?" There was an uncomfortable pause. "OH yehhh! We hunted some big woods back home," Dickie offered. "Well… why do you all have new equipment then? And… are you compass ready to travel in our woods?" They shuffled uneasily. "Yeh Ray! Don't go psycho on us, man! We have hunted so much, we thought we'd get new geah foh this trip. That's all!" Dickie's answer somehow didn't ring true but watching them chain smoke cigarettes might have affected their wind… I hoped .

Conversation around the dinner table bounced back and forth from one subject to another, much like a panic stricken deer fleeing for his life. "How many big old bucks ya got in this ahea (area)," Dick questioned. "Well, we really aren't too concehned… is the woods thick wheh we will be huntin'?" He responded back, even before I had answered the first question. "We hunt many different locations," I grinned, watching John attempt to stuff yet another forkful of food into those bulging cheeks. "We may have you hunting a swamp one morning and then…" The group exchanged worried looks. "Wheh should we shoot the deeh," Bob interrupted me. "Kin we shoot the small ones, too?" John started choking on goodness knows what but due to his physical makeup, I decided that attempting the Heimlich manouver might be detrimental to both him and me. After several minutes of facial color change and Mama arriving with a choice of five different deserts, John dislodged whatever he was unable to force down his throat and resumed with some pie. The interesting thing about the entire process was that neither Bob or Dick had displayed the slightest concern for the welfare of their friend and fellow hunter… almost as though they were used to such an occurrence.

The snow subsided overnight but left a fresh white blanket on the landscape for the first morning of the hunt. One of my guides and I had driven the crew out to one of our more productive areas where we had seen several big bucks during pre-season scouting. The terrain was small rolling hills, open hardwood ridges and several softwood belts by small brooks in the valleys. We thought that this would be a good area for hunters that we still had some doubts about. The day was just dawning as Dick, all gung-ho to head out disembarked from our van. The price tag dangled from his new compass as he did several pirouettes, turning to chase the spinning compass needle. "Which way is noth, Ray?" I restrained him to halt the turning and grabbed the compass as Bob and John looked on, scratching their heads.

"You're joking, right Dick?" I queried. "You told me that you

can read a compass. You can read a compass, can't you guys?" They all mumbled an affirmative and Dick smiled up at me. "We was just jerkin' youh chain, Ray. I meant which way is noth up heh in Canada!" I looked at my guide and shook my head. "I want to see you all back here by the fire at noon today. We'll boil the kettle and discuss what you saw. Now pay attention to this topo map and I'll give you your coordinates." I might as well have talked to the trees!

Rain started up by nine o'clock and by eleven thirty, that new blanket of snow had disappeared. My guide, Wayne and I sat by a roaring fire talking and listening for shots. We had our hunters in an excellent area with good deer numbers and the weather was co-operating as was the rut so we really expected someone in the crew to get an opportunity early. That didn't happen. By one o'clock, none of our hunters had returned to the clear-cut and our fire so I was beginning to get concerned. "I'm going into the woods to check on our guys, Wayne. You keep the fire going. If one of our hunters shows up, blow the van horn three times to signal me. If two show, double it and if all three show up, triple it so I'll know."

Within a hundred yards of the cut, I found our first hunter. John was sneaking along the perimeter of the tree line, quite comfortable. He could hunt the deer trails and keep the lighted edge of the cutover in sight at all times. I stopped and asked if he had seen the other hunters or any game. He hadn't seen the other hunters but had watched three does and a fawn go by and had spooked several grouse. He intended to hunt the remainder of the day in this area and would come out at dark. I moved on.

I followed a well-worn deer trail down through the first valley and found Bob sitting on a stump, huddled against the rain. He didn't even see me until I was right on top of him and then he did some-thing that blew my mind. He jumped up and ran away from me, almost in terror. "Bob, Bob! It's me, Ray!" With that he stopped and turned around, clutching his heaving chest. "Good Lohd, ya scahed me! I thought you was a beah!" I reassured him that most bears were denned up by now and besides, he carried a rifle. "Head on back to the fire and dry out," I suggested. I pointed him in the right direction and told him to stay on the deer trail. "It will lead you right to the cutover, just below where we've got the firehole." He waved sheepishly and headed off, casting furtive glances from side to side as he went.

I crossed several ridges before I heard the van horn signal that Bob was out but still saw no sign of Dick. As the ominous dark clouds gathered and the rain fell more intensely, I hurried my pace. This was big country, even for a New Brunswicker and if Dick had lost his bearings, or if he had lied about being compass ready… and I had strong suspicions that he could get himself into major trouble! I decided to hike across a small valley and try the hardwood ridge to the west. In the wet leaves of an open area in the ridge, I found tracks, human tracks that beat an erratic path west, then east, then south and north. There was no question that the tiny footprints were Dick's and either he was lost or hunting a style of still-hunt I had never seen.

I ignored the looping trail for the most part and increased my stride. Before long, I came across a blaze orange vest, lying crumpled in the leaves. A glove and a woolen toque came into view several minutes later along with a hunting jacket. I gathered them up and crested the next ridge. Below me on a plateau, turning about in circles with compass in hand stood a half-clothed hunter. His gun lay on the ground beside him and before I could reach him, he was staggering away from the gun, staring at the compass. "Dick, Dick!" I shook him by the shoulders. "Oh thank God! Ray, Ray… show me wheh noth is up heh in Canada again! I must have fohgot." I gathered his belongings, dressed him in his soaked clothing and instructed him to follow closely. That part of the order wasn't needed. He became my shadow for the rest of the week.

During that time, Dick learned many things about guns and the woods and the game he was hunting. Probably the first and most important lesson was not to point a loaded gun at your guide right after seeing a huge buck and two does cross your path. I was even more thrilled to find that he had taken the safety off and had his finger on the trigger. The second lesson involved deer scat. We were still hunting up into a hardwood ridge that displayed fresh deer sign everywhere when I heard a series of vicious coughs like someone clearing their throat or attempting to start up a dirt bike. I was visibly annoyed because I wanted these guys to bag a buck or two. I looked over and Dick was waving frantically. I walked over.

Dick stood there beside several large beech trees holding up several large round balls of moose scat. Eyes wide and mouth gasping, he looked at me. "I want this buck, Ray! I want this buck! What would a deeh like the one that cwapped this stuff field dress at?" I bit my lip and summoned my most solemn facial expression. "Dick, the animal that did this will field dress at a good six hundred pounds!" He shook his head incredulously. "Wow! My God! Let's get aftah him," Dick responded. "He'll be in evwey wecohd book in the countwy! I didn't know they gwew that big! Wow!" I started laughing at this point, almost uncontrollably! "Dick, if we ever find a buck that craps stuff this size, I'm hunting him myself! That's moose crap!"

Bob fired at a big buck that morning on the north face of the ridge but a large maple tree got in the way. John had followed Wayne into the woods in one of the valleys and emptied his rifle on a conglomerate of stumps and fallen logs that he swore was a buck's back and antlered head. That scared the living daylight out of poor Wayne who vowed not to venture back into the woods with such incompetent hunters. The week passed slowly with no deer taken but both Wayne and I were glad to see Friday arrive right on schedule.

Dick was quite a fellow I had learned. He supposedly had taken deer back home but I seriously doubted it. "Yeh, I'm quite a huntah back home. I know just wight wheh the deeh are gonna be! I'm psycho, ya know. Yep, back home they call me Psycho man… cause I know wheh to find them deeh!" I thought on his statement and just how appropriate the name "Psycho man" was for this guy… despite the obvious fact that he meant Psychic!

Dick had some strange characteristics and ways. When he first arrived in camp, he spotted our outhouse. We had built it prior to hooking up indoor plumbing at the lodge. He came over and whispered "Is that what I think it is?" I looked at him and replied in a whisper "Yeh, it is. Just don't try to flush it!" Well, I found out that he would not use the bathroom in the woods, not even when one day, he got sick with terrible stomach cramps and the "runs". He came to the fire hole at noon, almost doubled up in pain. "Ray, where can I go? I gotta go… bad!"

I quickly retrieved some toilet tissue from the van and passed it to him. He looked around the area and then asked again. "Well, where can I go?" Wayne and I shared a puzzled look. "You can go any where, Dick. There are no laws up here in our province that specify where you use the bathroom. Go back into the woods there somewhere and relieve yourself." Dick moved off and we didn't see him until nightfall.

As we sat at dinner, his place at the dining table was vacant. "Where's Dick," I questioned the guys. They looked at each other and smirked. Then they started laughing. "He's using the bathroom…

held it all day… just about died." The laughter became louder as I stared incredulously at them. "Dick won't sh… in the woods! Won't even take a leak out there!" They laughed until they cried and poor Dick finally arrived at the table looking kind of peeked and frail. "Dick, is that true? You won't use the bathroom in the woods?" "Well… I would… but I just can't! It's disgusting and besides… theh ain't no flush!"

That last dinner together gave me more insight into what guiding was like for me, especially when we had hunters in camp like Dick and his cronies. "I'm gonna write a book someday about all our hunting adventures and some of our hunters," I told them. "Yeh, well just make sho' if ya wite about us that you mention that I'm psycho! Yeh, that's me… Psycho Dick!" I assured Dick that the world would be warned or told, about the "Deliverance" gang, led by a guy called Psycho Dick!

Chapter 5
Bird Doggin' with Mack

Mack was a big, elderly man, probably six foot six, and he weighed in at somewhere near two hundred and forty pounds. He was also extremely hard of hearing and his left eye socket held a poorly made glass eye that looked more like a cat's eye marble than a human eye!

Although a man of obvious means, Mack was cheap or possibly miserly when it came to spending money on himself. The first autumn he came to bird hunt with us, he was having trouble adjusting to two new hearing aids. He complained that they were either too loud or not loud enough and he said they snapped and crackled in the rainy weather. "You should take them back to the company," I had suggested. He smiled craftily.

"Nahh! I didn't buy them, Ray. My cousin owned 'em first and then he died. Well, I went to his funeral service and walked up to pay my respects and my Gawd! I saw that they were gonna bury him with those two brand new hearing aids stuck in his ears. My old ones were on the blink and he had always bragged about these new ones he had got shortly before he passed away, so I stooped over the casket and popped 'em both out! He wouldn't be needin' 'em where he was goin!" I swallowed in horror and disbelief. "You're kiddin', right Mack?"

"Hell no! I slipped 'em in my top suit coat pocket and no one even knew! I wish he was still around though. I'd tell him what I think

37

of his damned hearin' aids!" I did not respond although I thought that I shouldn't expect a tip when his hunt was over!

An avid grouse and woodcock hunter, Mack had purchased a bird dog a couple of years prior to his hunting adventures with us and I must say, that bird dog lived a charmed life. Mack had re-named the dog Charmer (it was already a year old when he acquired it), and had spent several thousand dollars for it. He soon found that the dog was nowhere near being trained and proceeded to spend another several thousand dollars on dog obedience and training schools. Yep, you pinch some poor dead guy's hearing aids but spend thousands on a bird dog. Actually, the term "bird dog" fits many dogs and dog breeds but I have never encountered another dog that was less suited to the title than Charmer. If he is a bird dog, then I am truly a Leprechaun! You shall see what I mean as our tale progresses!

The first morning of the hunt found me chomping at the bit. I had told Mack about the bountiful supply of grouse and woodcock in our covers and not yet knowing his dog, looked forward to a day of wing shooting enjoyment. The morning dawned crisp and frosty and that amber autumn sun climbed lazily into an azure blue sky. It was a day fit for royalty and I sipped hot coffee while we headed for the first cover of the day. As we drove along an overgrown logging road, the first flock of birds wandered out in front of us. "Mack, look! There must be a dozen grouse or more, right here in front of the truck! Grab your gun and Charmer and let's have some fun!"

Mack disembarked slowly, much too slow for my liking, but Charmer bolted from the cab's back seat. As Mack fumbled with shells for his double barrel Parker twelve gauge, the dog did something I have never witnessed before. He charged straight into that massive flock of young grouse causing them to scatter. Some scurried into the underbrush while others flew up into the trees. Charmer, great bird dog that he was, continued his charge on down the logging road several hundred yards and didn't even stop for Mack's voice commands or the whistle. "Damned dog! It's because he's in new country; that's all!" Mack was apologetic.

"Well, let's bag a bird or two, Mack and see if we can get your dog to come back". Mack swung the shotgun and pointed it at a big grouse perched on an overhanging limb. Ka-Boom! The load of shot cut several branches off including the one the bird perched on. At first, I thought he had bagged it but before its plummeting body hit the ground, wildly flapping wings carried it off into the tree line.

Mack tried another grouse as it scurried along the ground but that load of shot just kicked up mud and leaves. One grouse actually came charging right across the road so close; it stepped on Mack's boot in its rush to be gone. Within a minute, the flock had vanished and all that could be heard was Mack's cussing. I was in a state of shock. We walked down the old road into the grown up, cut over area, ideal for birds and although we called for Charmer to come back, it was several hours later before the dog finally trotted in to our fire and dinner hole. Mack had connected with two grouse and a woodcock that I pointed out after missing several we had flushed earlier. "You don't need a dog, Mack when you have me," I grinned but I admit I was glad when Charmer came back that first morning. Mack shared his sandwiches with the critter and gave it a drink. "You're a good dog, Charmer," he stated and patted that ugly setter's head. "He'll do better next time Ray but I'm gonna put a beeper and shock collar on him anyhow!"

Since Mack was hard of hearing, he had a tough time keeping track of Charmer, the dog that had never been trained to hunt close. In fact, I had trouble containing the laughter as first the day and then the week progressed. Each time that Mack would let

Charmer out of the truck to hunt, Charmer would take off at high speed. Although he was supposed to be a "pointer", he seemed more at home being a long distance runner, a Greyhound rather than an English Setter, and finally after Mack had made up all the excuses for the dog's bad behavior, he decided to start shocking the dog so it would obey. Have you ever watched a distraught parent attempt to control a child who had never been disciplined in his life? Charmer couldn't understand the mild shock settings and the collar must have tickled. Mack would yell in his most authoritative voice. "Charmer, stop! Charmer, come!" If Charmer had fingers instead of toes, I am sure he would have flashed Mack the one finger salute as he totally disregarded commands... all commands!

Mack bagged a fat grouse one afternoon after I had taken several minutes pointing it out. The problem I finally realized was that I was on Mack's blind side pointing for his glass eye, so I hurried around to his good eye side and pointed to it! Charmer sat on a leash attached to the truck bumper. "Let him off so he can fetch the bird, Ray." I did as I was asked but Charmer was not impressed.

"Fetch the bird, Charmer! Fetch!" Mack pointed in the direction where the grouse lay, visible to all but the feeble minded. "They taught him to fetch well at obedience school. You just watch this, Ray! Now go and fetch the bird!" It was kind of like watching an Abbot and Costello movie. I gritted my teeth and pinched myself so I wouldn't laugh hysterically and possibly insult my client and friend. The dog wagged his tail and sat there looking at Mack. Several commands later, he still sat there. I was almost bursting but what happened next sent me over the edge.

Mack held the dog's head and looked deep into its eyes with his one good eye. "Now Charmer, I am only going to show you how to fetch just this once so you pay attention." With that incredible statement, Mack walked over to the tree line, bent down and grabbed the grouse, feathers and all, in his own mouth. He walked back and laid the bird in front of that stupid dog and I walked up into the woods behind the truck, shaking and crying with laughter that had been bottled up way too long! I didn't return for fifteen minutes, only approaching the truck when I was sure that I could control myself. "Got the runs… Mack. Had to go and had to go quickly," I lied. Surely the good Lord will excuse such an untruth, told to protect the feelings of a nice old man with the world's dumbest bird dog!

Toward the end of the week, the dog was starting to get on my nerves but something always happened to lift my spirits. Mack decided that Charmer needed a heavier shock to control him so he turned the remote control to the max. I watched him do it and despite not being fond of the dog, I still expressed my concern. "Oh it won't hurt him too bad! He's tough. He can take it!"

"Did you read the instructions that came with the shock collar, Mack?"

"No, but I've turned it up half way and only brought a squeal out of him. Don't worry, Ray. He's gonna listen to me today and when I get back home, I'm gonna take him in for more training. It's not that expensive, only eight hundred dollars for the month."

We drove to a cover area with alder swales and small islands of cedar. It was an area dotted by small to medium sized pools of water and small brooks and literally loaded with woodcock! Perhaps given the fact that Charmer had no idea what a grouse was or that he was supposed to point them out to us before scaring them off, and given that woodcock traditionally sit tight longer, he might do better. Yeah, right!

Mack let him out on his leash and fought him for several minutes until we thought he was calm and wouldn't charge off but as soon as Mack un-snapped the leash, away ran the dog. Mack stood there swearing angrily as I followed the dog's progress by the steady beep-beep sound. He circled a good half-mile area and stopped behind us to drink as he stood belly deep in a pool. It was at this moment that Mack decided to zap the dog after yelling himself hoarse. He pushed the button and the dog instantly went into spasms! I heard an ungodly yelping and some noises that I have never heard a dog make and watched as the animal writhed in the water. Its hair stood up and its floppy ears stood straight up as Charmer performed a dreadful water ballet. Mack was holding the button down and cussing as he screamed for Charmer to return to him. Personally, I had mixed emotions about the whole affair but never wanting any animal to suffer much, I rushed to Mack and yelled for him to release the button. Not hearing what I had said, he shook his head and replied, "I don't know where he is but he must be feeling that shock!"

I grabbed the remote and turned to point at the dog still quivering in the pool of water. Mack yelled for him. "Get out of that water now, Charmer and come here! First thing you'll ruin that new collar!" It was the first time all week that the dog obeyed. He came with his tail tucked and his eyes to the ground. Mack praised him, oblivious to what had just occurred. Fortunately, the poor dog survived the ordeal. Needless to say, I pointed and flushed several woodcock for Mack to miss and Charmer waited in the truck. I watched Mack half walk, half stagger to the truck. "It's that glass eye of mine," he offered. "I don't have depth perception anymore and I think it might have an affect on my shooting." "Maybe it does Mack," I comforted.

Just when I thought I had seen everything, something new would pop up. We were driving along an old back road one afternoon, heading for yet another grouse cover. As I drove, the dog stood half over me, peering out the window with his front paws resting on the back of my seat. I was annoyed but that soon changed to anger as drops of dog drool hit the nape of my neck. "Get back there, Charmer! Now!" I commanded sternly but the dog paid no more attention to my commands than Mack's. Mack had heard something and refusing to ask me to repeat it, he'd answer with what he thought might be a proper response.

"Yep, Charmer does love this bird hunting, don't you boy?"

The dog stuck his face out the window and sniffed the breeze and withdrew to drool down my back, totally ignoring me. Mack was peering out the window on his side of the truck as we drove along so the next time Charmer stuck his face out into the afternoon breeze, I pushed the power window button and the window crept up under that foolish dog's neck. There was a quick yelp and Charmer's legs flailed against the back seat as he tried to escape.

Mack had heard the sharp yelp, but once again, misinterpreted. "Yep, Charmer must have smelled a bird. Good dog!" I lowered the window and Charmer, slumped into the back seat. That was the end of him drooling on me and he never stuck his face up toward the window again. In fact, he sat in that back seat silently until we let him out for the next hunt. Once again, he decided to run off and once again, Mack yelled for him. Mack took a long looped leash and stood watching that hopeless dog race back and forth by us. The ground was extremely muddy here; soupy brown mud, and I could almost foretell what would happen next.

The dog came racing by once again so Mack tried to lasso him. This time, he did so but Charmer never even slowed down. He jerked Mack off his feet and dragged him through that mud and slime before Mack's weight slowed and then stopped him. "Charmer you no good son of a b...!" Mack screamed as he tried to stand. I stood motionless watching things unfold. Mack was covered in wet brown mud, even his face and wild bushy eyebrows were coated but the thing that kind of freaked me out was the big chunk of mud resting on his glass eye. I kept thinking he'd blink or squint and remove it but that didn't happen. He just stood there swearing at his prized bird dog. Finally, I suggested that he clean his eye in the truck mirror and we'd head for camp. Mack made up with the dog, lovingly fed him a treat and off we drove.

On the way back to camp, he told me how he loved hunting here, how he had enjoyed the scenery and how great Charmer had performed. I glanced into the rear seat toward the worst bird dog I had ever seen, a dog that had cost my friend a pile of money, a dog not worth the dog food he consumed each day, and then I glanced over at an old hunter, smiling thoughtfully through a muddy mask and gently praising his dog. "He hunted well, didn't he Ray," Mack grinned.

I shrugged and grinned myself. "Yeah Mack, I can truthfully say I've never seen a bird dog perform like Charmer, not in my wildest dreams! It was one fun week!" We drove the rest of the way in silence, with Charmer snoozing on the back seat. "I'd better close the window Mack. Charmer might smell a bird and try to go after him," I patted my old friend's shoulder. Yep, love really is blind and deaf as well!

Chapter 6
Stewie's Tiny Trophy

The buck looked at us briefly as we stood in the shadows of the swamp on that dark rainy afternoon in mid November. Wayne, a friend of mine who also guided for me pointed to the heavy racked ten pointer.

"Buck, and a big one," he hissed, motioning with an arm and looking in my direction. I had seen the animal seconds before he whispered but remained immobile, not wishing to spook it. Too late!

In a spray of wet snow and dead leaves the big animal left the cover of big cedars and black spruce and with two does in tow that we hadn't seen prior, charged into the open hardwoods, almost directly in front of Stewie, one of our hunters from the deep south. The deer rushed away from us and what they perceived as immediate danger but slowed to a fast walk when they came in front of Stewie. I waited for the roar of his rifle; a roar that never came.

I whistled loudly and caught Stewie's attention and motioned at the three deer walking just ahead and away from him at an angle. Good lord, a blind hunter could see them so why wasn't he shooting? That big old buck was Boone & Crockett material. Wayne moved close to me and whispered in disbelief. "What the heck is he doing? Why doesn't he shoot that buck?" We watched as Stewie waved at us and then both he and the deer disappeared from our view. We stood there scratching our heads.

To know why a deer hunter from the deep south who had

traveled all this way to our door didn't shoot that buck, you must have a small peek at Stewie and what made him tick. Stewie came to us the last week of our deer season some years ago as a guest of his father, a muscular, brawny retired Special Forces Officer. Stewie and his father Bert were as different as night and day. Bert was sixty-two years young while Stewie was forty-two years old. Bert had lived and breathed the wilderness and hunted all his life while Stewie had lived a bookworm sort of life, sheltered by a doting mother and only condoned by his father. Efforts on Bert's part to introduce him to hunting and fishing had failed and he had grave concerns about his offspring... even whether Stewie was indeed his offspring!

Stewie was medium in height, pot bellied, round shouldered, non-muscular to the nth degree with a tiny head, narrow eyes with coke-bottomed eyeglasses and always with a two to three day growth of beard. While his father dressed neatly and appeared well mani-cured and coiffed, Stewie always looked sweaty and greasy with a balding top knot and scraggly jet black side hair that sort of sprang out at you like the rim of a hat.

My first encounter with Stewie was quite memorable. Although I have field dressed moose, deer and bears and have had my hands in more fecal matter than I care to relate, I actually hesitated when he extended his hand in greeting. Perhaps it was the pungent odor of an unwashed body or that sweaty unkempt look which made me hesitate. It might also have been the heavy nasal whine he made when he talked but at any rate, I pretended to scratch my neck and finally shook his hand. Bert, on the other hand was no problem for me. Spotlessly clean and smelling of Old Spice he grinned as he came around the four wheel drive Jimmy and grasped my hand in his powerful grip. He was a man's man while Stewie... well we weren't quite sure what he was.

I offered to carry gear for the guys as we always do and while my son Terry grabbed a big pack, I latched onto a medium sized trunk. Good grief! The trunk must have weighed a hundred pounds and I struggled with it to get it through the lodge door. I found out later that Stewie carried around a portable library of books with him and like the famous credit card, he never left home without them! Perhaps I had been missing the boat for so many years, failing to include a trunk of literary works in my "need to bring to camp" list.

Stewie had grabbed a soft sided suitcase which came undone as he entered ahead of me. He walked casually to a corner bunk across the room with clothing falling and dragging behind him. "Stewie, your suitcase popped open and you are losing your clothing," I grinned.

He looked around as he set the half empty suitcase on his bunk and replied. "That's no problem, Ray. Don't worry about it. I'll get them later." At that point in time, another hunter came in and stepped a muddy foot on a pair of red woolen long johns. He stopped when he noticed and his mouth dropped as he surveyed the scattered clothing just lying there on the floor. "What happened," Dick asked, stepping back off the underwear.

"Oh, don't worry about it. I'll pick them up later," came the nasal whine.

I had serious misgivings about Stewie from the start. He told me he had been a land surveyor in California and assured me that I needn't worry about him in the big woods of New Brunswick. "I never worry when I'm in the woods, Ray. I've run lines and everything."

Bert sat quietly and listened to all that I said in camp and he especially paid heed to my compass bearings and reference points as we disembarked the first morning of the hunt. Dick did likewise but Stewie on the other hand, was preoccupied with digging through his eighty pound pack. Finally he emerged with a compass and without checking a bearing or direction, shoved it into his pants pocket. "You heard what I said, Stewie, right? These are big woods and you need to know directions and bearings. The nasal whine of "yeh, yeh," and a nodding head didn't ease my concerns.

The first morning of the hunt saw heavy rain and cold temperatures but there was no wind. Wayne and I had built a campfire and had a pot of black tea boiling on it when an excited Stewie burst forth from the treeline.

"Ray, Ray," he yelped frantically.

I jumped to my feet and hurried across the clear cut towards him. "What's wrong, Stewie?"

"A buck breathed at me! A buck breathed at me!" I bit my lip and surveyed the hunter.

"What are you talking about, Stewie? What does that mean and why didn't you shoot him? Why are you so out of breath?" The questions were too much for Stewie who held up his hands while he jumped around like someone who needed to pee!

He took a deep breath and started. "I was watching one of those deer trails and reading a novel… a western about this cowboy who-"

I stopped him with a brisk "get on with what happened" command. "Well, I looked up when I heard something coming down the trail and it was a buck with big horny things in its head. It stopped and looked at me and shook its head and breathed at me!"

"Okay, Stewie, it snorted at you so what happened next? Why are you out of breath and why didn't we hear a shot?"

He looked at me like I had hurt his feelings and blurted "Well I ran away! That thing was going to attack me! I heard it breathe so loud and it shook its horn things at me!"

"You've never hunted deer before, have you Stewie," I grinned.

"I've never hunted… anything," he stammered.

"Don't worry about it," I encouraged. "We'll make you into a hunter!"

As Wayne and I stood in the afternoon rain scratching our heads collectively and wondering why Stewie hadn't taken the shot at the big buck we had spooked toward him, we heard a shot on a distant ridge. It was Dick, our other hunter in camp polishing off a nice eight pointer. We took compass bearings and walked to the ridge to drag out the buck for Dick. Bert saw two small bucks and a doe but turned them down that afternoon.

As the last light of day faded, we finished the drag on Dick's deer and were loading it when I spotted a splash of hunter orange off in a massive clear cut. Bert had just arrived at the truck and we were expecting Stewie at any moment. Meanwhile, my guide Wayne remarked about the hunter in the middle of that massive clear cut. "Who would be stupid enough to be hunting way out there?" he queried.

"Goodness only knows! Probably one of those dumb northerners," I laughed. "Ain't been a deer out there since they cut that area last year. They'd have to pack a lunch just to go through it," I grinned.

Darkness came on and we sat in the warmth of the truck cab ridiculing the idiot who had sat in the middle of that clear cut, wasting a fine afternoon in deer season. Wayne responded with a "Can you believe anyone would be so stupid as to actually sit out there? I'll bet there isn't even a deer track out there!" "Yeah, somebody wasted their time making that baby," I laughed loudly. Bert and Dick had sat laughing along with us and joining in when suddenly Bert stopped and frowned.

"Don't suppose that was Stewie," he asked. You could have

heard a deer fart right then. Wayne and Dick and I stopped laughing and looked at each other as the awful question sunk in.

I cleared my throat and trying hard to lessen the impact of our ridicule, I turned to Wayne and said "Course you never know when one of those bucks is going to head out across that clear cut. Maybe that hunter knew something we didn't!"

Yeah, right! Within ten minutes, we saw someone approaching from the cut over and of course it had to be our man of the hour, Stewie. Bert shook his head and asked Stewie what he was doing out there.

"Well," came the grating whine, "Ray and Wayne waved me off this afternoon so I figured they didn't want me to hunt in those woods. I turned around and hunted through that big cut."

Bert was obviously embarrassed as we were and it was sort of awkward at that moment so I tried to ease the tension. "Did you see anything, Stewie," I queried.

"Nah, just a gopher. I think it was a gopher. You don't have squirrels that weigh twenty pounds or so… do you?" I bit my lip and tried not to look at Wayne who was staring at the floor of the truck and chewing on his own tongue.

"Did you see any sign, son," Bert hoped against hope.

"Nah, no tracks, no scat, but I figured you guys might scare something out to me."

"Speaking of that exact thing Stewie, didn't you see that buck and two does that ran over and stopped in front of you this afternoon when you saw us wave and point?"

Stewie looked at me for a moment and innocently asked "You guys saw deer?" We drove homeward in silence from that point on.

The culmination of my efforts to create a hunter out of a bookworm named Stewie came on Friday, the last day of the hunt. Bert had bagged a magnificent twelve pointer that would make the Boone & Crockett record books on Thursday morning and although we expected Stewie to be ecstatic about his father's success, he wasn't. In fact, I suspected that he was a bit… maybe a lot envious of his dad! I told him that I knew of an area where the deer feed heavily at this time of the year and he could hunt there come Friday morning. "You'll get him tomorrow, Stewie," I patted the poor guy's shoulder.

The last morning found Stewie in better spirits and raring to go so Wayne and I took him to a pie shaped area, with streams on both sides of two miles of prime forest. The streams eventually joined in the south and with the logging road forming the third side of the triangle, we felt confident that Stewie would do well in there. We gave him directions and he actually listened to them. I described the area and the feed lot with the small brook nearby and told him of a couple of major bucks I had seen when I had scouted it. Off he went with a slow, deliberate wave of the hand and Wayne set about gathering wood for a fire.

I waited and listened and a couple of hours into the morning hunt, I heard the heavy roar of a hunting rifle. "Stewie's fired at something," I grinned at Wayne.

Wayne cast a doubting eye in my direction across the crackling campfire and responded. "Yes! The question is what did he fire at? That man is the most incompetent hunter I have ever seen, Ray! Good Lord! He's so much different than his father!"

I took a sip of hot black tea with a wood ash floating in it. "Well, we'll see and we should see quite soon," I laughed.

An hour went by and then a second. Wayne looked at me and frowned. "Where is that man? Do you suppose he missed what he fired at?" It was yet another gray morning and the dark clouds were threatening rain once again. I started to respond to Wayne's questions when Stewie came bursting from the woods, right on the run. He yelled and waved frantically, running right on by us and the fire, so excited was he.

"My Gawd, I shot a monster, Ray! A monster! Huge! A monster!" He gasped for air and I instructed him to calm down. Sweat dripped from his red face and his eyeglasses were heavily steamed up. I was surprised that he had found the logging road at all.

Wayne grabbed a drag rope and gloves while I questioned Stewie. "Where did you shoot him?"

"Right in the as…!"

"No, no! I mean where in the woods did you shoot him?"

"By the vigorous brook!"

"Where?"

"By the vigorous brook! I shot him by the vigorous brook! You know!" Stewie seemed a bit agitated that I hadn't immediately recognized where he had downed this monster.

"What the heck is a vigorous brook," I asked, once again biting my lip. He explained the term and with several geographic questions later, I found that he'd have to take us to it.

"No problem," he replied in that whiney voice. "I marked the trail with ribbon all the way. It's an hour and a half walking time."

Wayne and I took a compass bearing and followed Stewie into the woods. Several hundred yards in, we seemed to be traveling in a large circle so I asked Stewie if he had circled. He assured me that he had not but we suddenly found ourselves at the center of a hub of ribbon trails. 'What the heck is going on," I shook my head. "Which trail leads to the deer?"

"Well, I'm not sure," he spun around twice. "I got a bit turned around and crossed my path a few times."

"I thought you were a surveyor down south," I pushed.

"Well, I was but they fired me!" I shook my head once again and Wayne who had sat down on a log in disgust looked up and asked. "What do we do now?"

I questioned Stewie again and finally got a familiar landmark birch knoll for a reference point. I took another compass bearing and forsook the ribbon trails and we walked straight up on his monster deer. I grabbed the front legs and lifted the huge animal skyward. "You shot this… this deer?" I snickered despite myself. "This was the monster, Stewie? It's a fawn… not more than seventy pounds! Why did you think it was a monster?" Undaunted, he stepped back and waved his arms excitedly. "That is a monster, Ray! It just looks small to you 'cause you're huge and built like a wrestler! We ain't all wrestlers, ya know!" He hung his head for a moment and muttered "It is huge and Daddy will be so proud of me!" Kind of hard to picture coming out of the mouth of a forty-two year old man and Wayne could control himself no longer. He rolled on the ground laughing uncontrollably as I stood holding the fawn with one arm and hand.

"I think I'm gonna like hunting," Stewie grinned. "Would you snap a picture of me and my trophy, Ray?"

"Yeh, I'll do that Stewie… and maybe you can get it enlarged!" With that, Wayne and I spent a week's wages of pent up frustration on mirth and we both rolled the ground in tears of laughter! I carried Stewie's monster deer out of the woods on my shoulders but his dad was as pleased as punch with what Stewie had bagged.

"I know it's not big Ray, but just remember who bagged it," Bert patted my shoulder.

"We all have our own cross to bear, Bert… though yours seems a bit on the heavy side," I replied, but I was glad that the father and son went home happy.

Chapter 7
Pirate Pete
or The Machine Gun Kid

The impatient knock on the cabin door was both sharp and hurried and had barely brought me to my feet when it was repeated. I walked to the door and opened it partially to stare at a small group of bear hunters led by a swarthy middle aged man with a camouflage bandana tied around his head. They were all fully outfitted in camo and all looked a bit unkempt but it was this one particular fellow, minute in stature with a small pot belly and beady little weasel eyes that commanded my gaze. "Yes, can I help you gentlemen," I grinned. "Ya know damned well ya can help us… if you're Ray Dillon… the outfitter. You are him aren't ya?"

It was the little guy who had responded, shuffling his feet all the while with those sunken weasel eyes darting about nervously. I invited the hunters in and offered to unload their gear but the nervous little guy Pete declined the offer for all of them. "We'll carry our own gear. Thanks just the same," he shot back in a slightly agitated manner. The three hunters with Pete were regular fellas or so they seemed but there was no question of who ruled the roost in this group. Although Pete was only half the size of the other guys, his sharp tongue and authoritative demeanor sent them scurrying about like rats on a sinking ship.

"You, Freddie, grab that beer out of the cooler and put it in the fridge and you, Sammy, bring my gear in here and stick it in the private room on the right. Bill… ahh… bring in my guns and don't bang 'em on anything and you… guide… tell me what I need to know about bears!" I had been grinning up to that point but ol' Pete just took away all my humour when he started ordering me around.

I towered over this guy who wasn't much bigger than Papa Smurf so I stooped and looked him square in the eye. "Well… the first thing you need to know about bear hunting at my camp is that you never, never refer to me as "you… guide!" The second thing you need to know is that you are hunting with me and although you may have paid me to guide you, you didn't pay me to take your crap, and the third thing you definitely need to know is that black bears are dangerous critters, they can and occasionally do hunt you, and you will stay healthy only by staying in my good graces! Got that?"

Pete swallowed hard and looked deep into my eyes. They say you can see a man's soul through his eyes and that Sunday afternoon, Pete saw the good and pure side of my soul and… the black and evil side that I keep subdued most of the time. From that moment forward, Pete changed his attitude toward me.

We spent the evening by a crackling fire with me dispersing advice and large amounts of black tea, hot coffee and the occasional beer. "You can have drinks in the evenings after the hunt but no getting plastered and come morning, you all better be stone cold sober. Understand?" The others had witnessed my address to their boss so everyone nodded vigorously. That night, I took great pleasure in telling them stories of hunts that had gone horribly wrong and of vicious bear attacks and I demonstrated on a live mount bear we had at the cabin how important it is to make the proper shot. When I said my goodnights and headed for the house, I grinned as I walked in the cool mid-May night air. "I think I might have spooked 'em," I laughed!

During the spring bear season, the hunters have time for themselves in the mornings and early afternoons. They can fish or tour the wilderness, drive into the city or simply sleep in. We busy ourselves with preparing for the late afternoon-evening hunt doing up baits, making sure we have adequate cover and attractant scent in our packs. Also, that first morning, we visit the range with our clients. This crew was memorable on our stop at the rifle range. I have never seen a crew of hunters shoot like these guys. Never!

Bill was first man up and possibly the most normal looking and acting of the group. He fired one shot and then a second grouping them neatly in a one inch diameter. "How's that, Ray?" he inquired as the others busied themselves with adjusting rifle straps and ear protectors. "Wouldn't be too bad, Bill, if it had hit that sixteen inch square target. No, you need to bring that neat grouping onto the paper and preferably near the center of the target… not in the top left corner of the plywood backstop!" Bill was also the best shooter amongst the group. It would take too long to narrate the two hours we spent on the range but I will say that the group pock marked the surrounding area, cut off tree branches and continually pointed gun barrels at things they shouldn't, including each other. After the final shot was fired and the final score was in, I concluded that a black bear would be safest within the shooting crosshairs of these boys. And the final irony came when Pete swaggered up to inform me that he had decided to take his bear with the bow!

My guide, Dave and I loaded the motley crew and started dispersing them at their bait sites around mid afternoon, after several return trips to camp for seat cushions, a hunting license and Sammy's ammunition. Sammy, tall and gangly with two large protruding buckteeth in front, was first man on stand. That in itself should have been a relatively simple task but wasn't! Dave and I carried Sammy's gear down the trail and both of us were panting when we arrived at the stand site. It was just a short ten-minute hike from the road but we had struggled with two full packsacks that each weighed eighty pounds. "Sammy, what the heck you got in these packs," I queried as we arrived at the base of his tree. "Ah, just the basic survival stuff. You know, a hunter can't be too cautious when he's in the big woods up here in New Brunswick… And I'll be here until dark tonight!"

He proceeded to open one of the packs and the first thing he hauled out was a four-man tent, complete with pegs and folded post frame. He then brought forth a survival blanket, two large flashlights, and a Coleman lantern. Candy bars, several bags of potato chips and a six pack of sodas followed. "I thought I might get hungry," he surmised. We placed most of the food and gear in the packs including several Outdoor Life magazines and a book about Killer Bears and Dave mumbled in a low voice "Do you want all that stuff up in the tree stand, Ray?"

"Hmmm, no! That stand is only rated for three hundred pounds and besides, with all this food, it might help bait the bears in if it is at the base of the tree." We left the big packs resting against the tree trunk and gangly Sammy perched at the top.

A few miles later, we unloaded Freddie and placed him in a ground blind and on down the road, we transferred Bill. Freddie was a humungous man with a huge beer belly that overhung his belt, and the only way we could determine that he had a belt was by seeing a large bowie knife and a long flashlight dangling from somewhere under that belly. A tree stand would have been out of the question for Freddie to use since we barely got him fitted into the ground blind. Now, being a fairly big lad myself, I am not about to poke fun at someone with a weight problem but I do have to say that Freddie was a crowd! He was a policeman back home and I'm sure could have surrounded a building, all by himself! And I'm not even going to suggest the connection between policemen, donuts and weight problems. No sir! I'm not going to "be-little" this guy. He was a walking poster boy for the "eat smart, stay healthy" crowd.

Freddie walked the entire distance to his blind in just under thirty minutes; something that impressed me since Dave and I could cover the three hundred yards from the truck to the blind with forty pounds of bait each in ten minutes. We left Freddie huddled in the blind munching on a candy bar that he told us was to replenish his blood sugars and energy level.

Bill was a quick fix for us and as I mentioned earlier, the most normal looking of the bunch. We had him on stand in ten minutes and finally bumped down the old road with Pirate Pete leaning over the front driver's seat, camo bandana on head, dressed fully in camo and impatient as ever. "Just put me out there and don't come back till it's pitch black dark," he spewed.

"We'll be through to check on all you guys from time to time so if you need us for anything, just come out to the road and wait," I informed him. I had seen his kind many times over. The old "just drop me in the woods and don't come back for a week" comment usually spells big trouble for us because it is normally made by those most inept at hunting and most fearful of the big woods.

Bill grabbed bow and arrows and followed us to his stand. "Ain't high enough," he shook his head as he surveyed the wooden home made platform some fourteen feet in the tree. He scrambled up the two by four wooden ladder and leaned over the wooden railing to peer down at me. "This thing should be up there twenty five feet or so. Have ya actually taken bears from this height?"

Dave looked at me and we shared a knowing look. I smiled and stated that we take bears regularly from the ground. We left him there unpacking his gear and hanging up his bow. As Dave and I drove down the road, I told him we would need to come back within two hours. "He'll be out at the road," I grinned. In two hours, we came back down the road and found Pete pacing back and forth, wide eyed and sweating profusely. He waved frantically when he saw the van coming and didn't wait for us to arrive. He ran several hundred yards toward us full tilt and had the side door open before I could stop the vehicle. "Are you okay Pete," I asked, genuinely concerned about his labored breathing and frightened, wild looks.

"Take me back to get my rifle," he blurted out. "Ain't gonna hunt with this bow no more." On our way back to the lodge, he explained. Apparently the first bear showed up within twenty minutes of us leaving. He shot an arrow at the critter, and then another and another. All three missed and buried themselves in the ground. The bear took some bait, unperturbed and left. A second bear came in fifteen minutes later but Pete had been too afraid to come down to retrieve the arrows he had shot so he only had two arrows left. He buried both of them in trees around the bait site but didn't touch the second bear. With no arrows and a bear still at the bait, he freaked. He broke branches off the tree he was in and yelled and threw them at the bruin. Wondering what all the ruckus was about, the bear finally walked off and Pete scampered down and out the trail to the road.

Dave and I listened and bit our lips but saw a new Pete emerge from the lodge carrying a semi-auto 7 mm Magnum rifle. He sort of swaggered that short pot bellied frame, squaring his shoulders and trying to suck in that gut to no avail. "I'll fix any bear that shows up now!"

We delivered him to his stand an hour later and told him to hunt until dark. At twenty minutes to dark, we sat just up the road and heard three shots. We drove down to the trail and disembarked, ready to go in and collect his bear but just then, three more shots rang out. Pete had fired at two bruins that evening and missed them both, making it four bruins he had missed that very first day of the hunt.

He was frustrated by his efforts and I was flabbergasted! "That gun shooting straight," I queried an obviously upset Pete.

"Well, you was at the range when we sighted in," he blurted. "Damned guns are unpredictable anyhow," he mumbled. I thought back to our sighting in episode and shook my head. As we drove homeward I thought, I hoped things would improve.

On Tuesday evening, Pete saw and fired at two bears while Bill bagged his bruin. "Hey Ray, you know that trick about having your shootin' pattern centered on the paper really works! I just centered those crosshairs and kept shootin' and I hit that old bear four times!" He was obviously excited and the bear was shot up so bad that he'd be lucky to have a hand towel made from the hide, let alone a full rug. Oh well! He was one happy bear hunter and that was more than you could say for the other hunters at the end of the week.

Sammy spooked off several bruins during the week while reading magazines he carried up into his tree stand and on one occasion while reading the book "*Killer Bears*", almost fell from the stand when a squirrel sneaked up to a limb beside him and started chattering. "Whew, I thought my time had come and if I hadn't had that safety harness on, it would have!" We smiled when we heard about this incident and just shook our heads when he spooked off bruins, night after night.

By mid-week, Freddie's ground blind looked like a landfill and we actually had to carry out a garbage bag full of food wrappers. He had seen a couple of bears too but on both occasions, was eating some sticky gooey food and never got his hands cleaned off fast enough to grab his gun. I don't honestly believe it would have mattered anyhow since on Thursday afternoon while carrying his gun in to his blind, I noticed his scope was partially blocked by some foreign substance that could have been processed sandwich meats on one end. I stopped and cleaned it out for him but still had a blurred image when I looked through it. The other end had some syrupy material splashed across the lens and part of a crushed banana in the chamber, mashed up against the firing pin. I passed it to him and warned him to clean it up as I left the area. "Oh yes, and for goodness sakes, check to see there isn't anything in the barrel," I cautioned.

On the last evening of the hunt, Pete got an early start on scaring off bears. At 5 p.m., we heard the first shot and at 6:30 p.m., the second and third. At 9 p.m., just a half hour before last light, there were three shots from his bait site and when we drove up to pick him up (he was out by the road fifteen minutes before dark) a huge boar bear started to cross the road a mere forty yards distant. I grunted and the bruin stopped to sniff the air. He was broad side. "Take him Pete," I whispered. Ka-Bang! Ka-Bang! Ka-Bang! Ka-Bang! The bear stood still for all four shots despite two alders being cut in two, off to one side of the road fairly near the animal and gravel being sprayed from another shot thirty yards further down the road. We weren't sure where the fourth shot hit but the bear was safe. He sniffed again and walked off into the bush. Dave was standing beside the truck as this all transpired. In a gruff strained voice that was fighting back uncontrollable laughter, he laid his hand on Pete's shaking shoulder. "You comin' back here bear huntin' next year," he questioned.

"Yeh, no question! I fired at eleven bears this week, man!"

"Then, I suggest that you bring a machine gun, Pete," Dave grinned.

Chapter 8
Otis Shanks -
Licensed New Brunswick Guide!

Otis Shanks had been a guide in his younger years; not a good one but a bona-fide licensed New Brunswick Guide none-the-less! His reputation for guiding was all too well known by his peers in the small community of Hamstrung where we lived. I found Otis standing on a railway track in hunting season one fall, staring intently into the woods off to one side. He cut quite a figure standing there, mouth agape, huge belly overhanging a pair of belted military combat pants, combat boots shined to the highest degree of shine and combat jacket wide open, unable to cover that enormous gut. He didn't acknowledge my approach, not even when I came close by and stopped to look in the same direction as Otis. Otis stood and stared, sipping a cold beer. "What do you see," I whispered staring at I knew not what.

"Nothing," came the reply, "but there could be a deer in there behind those trees."

"Did you hear something," I asked still staring.

"No… why?" I started giggling like a school girl and after those tense moments staring at the woods and nothing else, I laughed loudly. Otis turned and surveyed me as I stood there laughing uncontrollably and extended a stubby fingered hand. "I'm Otis, former military man and now a professional guide, and you would be…?" I shook his outstretched hand and introduced myself.

I should have said "My name is Ray and I will eventually find that I am the stupidest outfitter, ever." That's right, folks, it was me during one of my stupidest moments and although I should have clued in on this extraordinary mushroom fodder artist, I didn't, preferring to think the best of my fellow man. We talked, became friends and I hired him to guide for our operation… minus the beer that he so loved to drink, of course! Oh Lord, when I think back over the years!

Otis had been in the military and worked his way in forty years from private to… semi-private? No, just kidding! He actually became a Corporal numerous times and eventually became a Sargeant – numerous times! I believe he was the only soldier issued "Velcro" stripes because the army knew that he would only go so long and do something totally stupid and get busted back down to his original rank! Well, he brought this masterful intelligence to me and being the kind, gentle hearted critter that I am, I failed to see or possibly admit his true IQ for many years. I would not kid you! He had an IQ of 22 and a common fieldstone or rock has an IQ of 23!

To let you see just a glimpse into the world of the totally inept, I'll relate some of the things that happened to us as we traveled the woods together. Although Otis had been in the army for so long, and carried an impressive compass, he never could comprehend its purpose. He also liked to impress us with his amazing knowledge about any and every subject. "Did you know that when you are driving one of our military trucks in a convoy, each vehicle behind the first must drive five miles per hour faster than the one in front of it to keep up?"

"Well that's preposterous Otis! If you were eight vehicles behind, according to your theory, you would have to drive forty miles per hour faster than the lead truck to keep up. Wouldn't take long for you to run into or over the whole darned convoy!"

"No… you're wrong!! You "civi's" just don't understand what we military guys do!" I shook my head and laughed hysterically in disbelief that the good Lord had allowed Otis time on earth with regular people. I was glad he had never married and procreated!

On one occasion that I remember well, we had spring bear hunters with us. Otis drove my old van with several hunters inside. He had baited this particular area and supposedly knew it well so when he stopped ahead of my 4x4 Chevy truck and came back for a bait bucket and the hunter's tree stand, I helped him unload it and walked in through the woods toward the site. We came to an open area but I was concerned, having spied no trail, no bear sign and no broken branches or foliage. The hunter followed Otis and now stood in this small opening several yards behind my guide. I walked by and over to where Otis stood, mouth agape. "Where is the bait," I asked. "Ahhhh…" I knew our hunter had to be wondering about this. I lowered my voice and demanded again, in a firm, stressed voice. "Where is the bait you've been tending every day for the past three weeks?"

"Ahhh… I dunno Ray… maybe the bears moved it," he offered still gaping and looking around.

What can you do in such a situation? Here is a bear hunter who has scraped and saved to come to New Brunswick for the bear hunt of a lifetime and the village idiot has lost his bait site, a site he has tended every day for the past three weeks. I thought fast and cleared my throat. "No Otis, I don't think we should set him up here. The bears have taken this bait bucket. Let's take him to that hot new site down the road and set him up there, okay?" Otis looked as puzzled as he ever did, nodded and followed us back to the road. "Sorry about that," I grinned at the hunter. "Otis has some strange notions sometimes and doesn't let me in on them until the last minute. Had I known what his plan was, we would have never even walked down in there! We would have went to the new site that's getting all the action!" Whew! My hunter thought it a bit strange but he accepted the explanation. As Otis loaded the bait bucket back in the truck and the hunter climbed into the van up ahead, I whispered or perhaps quietly shrieked, "You better find that darned bait site, you idiot, and we'd better make sure he gets a bear!"

Forty yards up the road, Otis spotted the trail that lead to the real bait site and before the week was out, thank the good Lord, our hunter bagged a huge boar bear! This ongoing saga of Otis and the bears read like a "Ripley's Believe it or Not" book. I asked Otis to get someone to help him service our baits because the bears weren't hitting like they should one spring so Otis went and called one of his old army buddies, another Corporal by the name of Cleetis Hopper. Have you ever noticed that people of the same ability sometimes hang together in packs? Cleetis was almost on par with Otis. One morning, I gave them ten pounds of bacon and instructed them to visit each bait site. "Cook up some bacon at each site, splash the bacon grease around the site and hang the cooked bacon strips in the surrounding trees." Their orders were specific and simple and even an idiot couldn't go wrong on them… or could he?

I serviced another twenty baits in another area we hunt and by mid afternoon, arrived back at the lodge, hot, tired and happy to be home. By eight o'clock that evening, I was getting concerned about the duo of licensed guides I had entrusted. At nine p.m., I was ready to jump into my 4x4 to go looking for them and they drove into the yard. They were both paunchy big guys so the sweat on their brows didn't impress me. After grilling them on why they were late, I invited them into the lodge for supper. They both groaned and came back with "we couldn't eat another bite." Immediately, a red flag came up. "Why aren't you hungry," I asked. Otis looked kind of sheepish and shuffled back and forth from one foot to the other, a move I hadn't witnessed since a field trip to the zoo. Cleetis started doing the same little dance and both hung their heads. Good Lord! They started doing this shuffle in unison, sort of like a gorilla chorus line! It was disturbing to see such a spectacle but now I knew something was definitely in the wind and I knew it wasn't bears!

"You did visit each bait, didn't you Otis?" "Yahh…" came the reply and his gaze dropped to the ground. "Well, you did do the bacon burns and splash the grease around and you hung the bacon strips in the trees… right?" More uneasy shuffling and this time several gulps and some throat clearing from both guides.

"Well… We did cook the bacon up and we did splash the grease around… but…we… hmmmm… ate the bacon." The last part of his statement was almost inaudible but my disbelieving ears heard it anyhow.

"What! There was ten pounds of that stuff! You guys ate TEN POUNDS of BACON… TODAY… besides those picnic basket sized lunches you carried?"

Otis held onto his protruding gut and moaned… "but we'll never do that again… it was just that the bacon smelled so good and you know, its kind of like those potato chips. You can't eat just one!" I should have been furious but instead, I cried with laughter!

Over the years, things went horribly wrong at times, thanks to the competency of Otis Shanks. One morning in deer season, I found Otis asleep in the van. We had deer hunters in the woods nearby and Otis' simple task was to listen for shots and then help retrieve the downed buck for the client. I had rushed off to town to get supplies and while there, I picked up a twenty piece bucket of Kentucky Fried Chicken and a dozen Tim Horton's donuts. I had dropped by the fire hole where we planned to dinner before going off to scout another deer area. This was an area that I hadn't scouted since early fall. I wanted to see if it was receiving much activity now that hunting season had started. I woke Otis and left the donuts and chicken with him, telling him to start a fire and boil a kettle of tea and I would rejoin him sometime around noon. "Now stay awake and listen for shots," I insisted as I drove off.

Around half past twelve, I was still working my way across a hardwood ridge but I was seeing some good deer sign and more importantly, buck scrapes and rubs. It took me another fifteen minutes to get back to the truck and another twenty minutes to arrive at the dinner hole. Otis sat on a camp chair gazing into the fire as I drove up but got up immediately and seemed a bit nervous. "Hear any shots," I questioned.

"No… no shots this morning but the hunters all came out at noon. Yep, all four of them came out for lunch and just went back to the woods a few minutes ago." I thought that strange since those guys hadn't come out of the woods on Monday or Tuesday until dark. I asked if they had seen any deer sign or possibly some deer but Otis just coughed and said "I didn't ask them and they didn't say." I was ravenously hungry as only you can get from being in the great outdoors and some of those donuts and chicken would taste awfully good right about now. I walked over to the van and grabbed the KFC bucket but it was totally empty.

"Where did the chicken all go," I asked Otis who was doing the primate shuffle again. Otis looked at the ground and blurted out that he had been eating a piece of the chicken at noon when the hunters came by and they had helped themselves. I mumbled a bit angrily that they could have saved me at least a piece or two but consoled myself with the thought of having some donuts and tea. I reached behind the seat and brought out an empty donut box. Now, I was really angry. "Well, where the heck are the donuts, Otis? Don't tell me they ate all of them too!"

"Hmmm, hrummmph. Well I ate a couple," he stammered. Just then we heard a shot from the ridge adjacent to our position so I took a compass bearing and Otis and I headed in that direction.

Fifteen minutes later on a leaf strewn ridge, we came upon one of the hunters bending over a huge ten point buck. I dressed the animal out and we started to drag it. "Man, I'm hungry," I panted as we strained under the two hundred pounds of deer.

"Me too," said our hunter. On our way out, we encountered another of the four man crew sitting on a log with a sandwich and a drink.

"Just stopping for some lunch," he smiled. I looked at Otis who was really staring at the ground but I remained silent until we got back to the fire hole.

I cornered Otis by the tail gate of my truck and tried to look him in the eye; something which would have only been possible if you were a worm on the ground. "There were no hunters out at noon, were there Otis," I asked him.

"Noooo…" he replied in a low voice.

"You ate all that chicken and all those donuts, didn't you Otis," I grilled him. "Hrummmph… yes boss," he whimpered. "I was so hungry and they tasted so good and I had to eat to stay awake and… I'm sorry boss! I'll buy you more if you want!" He seemed so pathetic that I couldn't stay mad at him. I shook my head and grinned. It was my fault after all. You don't turn a ravenous child loose in a candy store without supervision nor do you leave chicken and donuts in the charge of someone who can't control himself.

Otis was very popular with the hunters in camp because they thought his antics and tribulations were intentional. He was the only bear guide I have ever met who was actually terrified of bears and one afternoon when we were carrying bait to one of our bear stands, we encountered a big sow bear with two cubs. Otis dropped his bag of bait and rushed by me heading to the truck the fastest I ever saw him move. The big sow stood on her hind feet sniffing the air and trying to see what all the commotion was about so I backed off as well but when I got to the truck, Otis had the doors locked and wouldn't let me in. I had to threaten the guy to get him to open the truck door and let me in. "What the heck were you thinkin'," I asked angrily.

"I was wonderin'… Ray… I knew I really didn't have to outrun that bear. I just needed to outrun you!"

I fired up the old 4x4 and headed homeward, wondering in my heart of hearts about the question that has haunted me for years. "Do people really need guides and if so, how did Otis ever get away with being one?"

Chapter 9
Did Someone Call SWAT?

"Dismount," barked the Sergeant as he gingerly stepped outside and flung open the sliding door of the van. Several hunters hurriedly disembarked, rushing to form a perimeter around the van and along the old dirt road and all the while, loading 12 gauge shells into their shotguns. It was quite a sight! I sat motionless but smiling as those six hunters, dressed in Swat Team black took up various positions in the immediate area. Some knelt down while others sprawled, all facing the thick belt of small trees and brush where their quarry had entered. They stared intently at the impenetrable thickets and the Sarge whispered loudly to his buddies. "See anything?"

"No, not me!" "Not me!" "No, me neither!" was the rapid response.

"Jake, sneak up on that left side and we'll cover ya," Sarge whispered. Jake, a tall wiry fellow with a handle bar mustache and a furrowed brow scampered over the slight knoll and up alongside the thicket. He shook his head viciously indicating that nothing was visible to him. Another couple of minutes went by as the tense standoff continued.

I looked in disbelief as I watched this drama unfold. Suddenly, a small brown, gray and black feathered bird sauntered from the cover and crossed the road some thirty yards distant. "There he goes guys… he's ahead of you on the road," I yelled. The ruffed grouse cast a knowing eye at these men in black and broke into a trot head-

ing for cover as six shotguns roared. Multi-coloured autumn leaves shivered in the barrage of bird shot and floated earthward as clumps of grass and dirt leapt skyward. I sat in the driver's seat in the van and bit my lip. "My goodness guys, you let a bird with a brain the size of a BB outsmart you!" They came back and mounted up, blaming each other for not spotting and taking the bird. It was the start of what would be a long and unforgettable week in camp.

Sarge was the leader of this group, a "by the book" drill Sergeant who had brought his swat team buddies along for a fall black bear hunt in New Brunswick. He was a good looking fellow with a rugged build that indicated years of dedication to physical training. He had nothing I could single out as an odd physical feature so I determined he might be reasonably normal. His buddies were also reasonable looking guys, sort of Marlboro Man types, who all had the stern sincerity of countenance that made me appreciative that I was one of the good guys.

Every one of them smoked big cigars and partook heavily of the elixir known as Jack Daniels in the late evenings back in camp.

Brave men all in the face of danger back in the big city, they were almost terrified in the dense woods of our province as daylight faded each evening. Excuses came fast and furious as one of my guides and I hustled around to pick up the hunters. "Ahh, I couldn't see another minute in them woods," one fellow told me. Hmmmm, it was an hour before dark when he came out to the road. "Feelin' powerful sick tonight," says another as we load him in, all the while munching on an apple, and "I came out to use the phone but I guess there ain't none around here, huh" was another's lament. Let me see now, we are twenty eight miles back in the woods and haven't seen a house, a power line, or another vehicle since we left the outskirts of civilization so NO, there won't be any phones.

I could see that our only hope of bagging bruins would be if they came to the bait sites early, preferably in late afternoon. We drove homeward and I considered our options.

Next day, I doubled the scent lures, did what we call bacon

and honey burns and encouraged our SWAT team to stay later. "Remember guys, you are here after black bears and they are usually quite shy critters that show up just before or right on the edge of darkness."

"Do you suppose they'd be crossing the roads earlier," one fellow asked "because if they do, I'll volunteer to sit out in that old field and watch the road for 'em." At that suggestion, all six hunters volunteered.

"No, we gotta go into the woods, guys. Now bears won't hurt you and you are all armed with high powered rifles so you don't even need to carry those shotguns in to the stands. You won't need 'em!" I was wasting my breath. Tuesday evening saw bears come in on four stand sites, all before six p.m. Three of the SWAT team bagged bruins while the police sniper missed a huge boar at thirty yards. Hmmm. Would someone please remind me not to call him if I'm ever taken hostage! Sniper all right! We gathered our bruins and drove homeward with an encouraged and hopefully braver group of guys that night.

Wednesday morning saw our group riding the roads for grouse once more and the Sarge told me he just wanted to bag one for mounting. "Just one," he grinned "so guys, if we see any, let me have first crack at 'em."

Within an hour, we came upon the first "Ruffie" and Sarge bailed out, almost before I got stopped. The grouse knew something was up and started running through the light underbrush. Sarge had taken time to once again load his gun full. He charged into the mixed growth and we heard several shots and some cussing. Then we saw the bird rush out to the edge of the tree line some fifty yards distant. "Hey Sarge, he's back out here," one of the guys yelled. "Want me to snuff 'em?"

"Nooo," roared a voice from the thicket. The Sarge busted through into the open some thirty yards beyond the bird and looked about. "Up here Sarge," our sniper yelled and pointed but by the time Sarge focused and reloaded his empty gun, the bird was gone. He unloaded the weapon and climbed into the van, pouting slightly. "Well, next time, just chamber one round and forget about cramming it full. You only need one shot and don't charge through the brush shooting," I instructed. Within minutes we rounded a bend in the road and there sat a plump grouse on the shoulder in the sunlight. Sarge jumped out and chambered a round as his buddies cheered him on from the back seats. "Take 'em Sarge, take 'em" was the chant as Sarge sneaked ahead several yards towards the motionless bird. He raised his gun and aimed, lowered it and decided to close the thirty yards between him and the bird.

The crew now chanted "Shoot him, shoot him, and shoot him Sarge!" At that moment the grouse became suspicious of this "black fatigues"-clad creature approaching and took to the air, heading right toward Sarge. Sarge screamed almost like a girl and raised the gun, whirling around as the grouse thundered past him and straight at the van and us! The crew who had been chanting "Shoot him; shoot him," were now yelling "Duck guys, duck!"

Ka-Wham! Birdshot hit the van's windshield and thank the good Lord it was 7.5 shot. I sat there, eyes bulging, hands grasping the steering wheel in a tight white knuckled embrace. The windshield looked as if it had a severe case of acne but both it and we were still in one piece. The grouse had flown the coop and Sarge came charging up, all apologetic and concerned. "Gosh Ray, I'm sorry, so sorry! We'll get ya a new windshield, buddy! It was that damned grouse's fault! He attacked me! Did you see that, flew right at me!"

We drove on albeit without a clear view of the road ahead.

Finally, we saw a bird and Sarge got out and blistered it. He grinned like a schoolboy as he came across the open field with his prize. "I'm gonna get this mounted, guys. Look at him, a big beautiful old… What did you call the males, Ray?"

"A drummer," I smiled. Just then, Sarge dropped the bird on the ground. He bent over to retrieve the big drummer with the beautiful tail feather fan but as he did so, he lost his balance slightly and stepped forward. Almost in one motion, he scooped up the bird but it no longer looked so impressive. Under his foot lay the tail fan, torn away from the bird when he clutched it up.

He held it up and grinned "I'm gonna still get this mounted, fan or not! Hey Ray, can a taxidermist glue that fan back on?" I just shook my head.

Several stops later, five of the six hunters had their birds and it was at this point that my son came along in my 4x4 truck. "Son, Billy hasn't got a bird yet, so you take the van and see if you can get him one on the way back to camp." He agreed and I drove off to do some other chores. As Terry drove the guys homeward, they razzed Billy about not bagging a bird and he was not taking it well. Now, as the van came over a knoll in front of a farmer's house, Billy yelled "Stop!" Terry slammed on the brakes looking for the dog or cat or child in the road but there was none. Billy had bailed out and was now aiming at a grouse sitting off to the side of the road, not twenty yards from the farmer's front porch where both the farmer and his wife rocked peacefully in the ambience of an early October morning. They stopped rocking and peered out at the burly swat team member as he leveled his shotgun… and in their direction. Terry rolled down his window to yell but it was too late. Billy's shotgun roared and the farmer and his wife dived for cover. The shot blew the bird right onto the farmer's lawn and my son rushed out past a grinning

Billy to gather up the bird, apologize to the farmer and his wife and to get the heck out of there. "We could have all ended up in jail dad," Terry confided later. "I was so scared when I saw him do that, and him a policeman!" I shook my head.

Later on that afternoon, we mounted up once more for the evening bear hunt. I dispersed the hunters and checked some baits and around five p.m., heard a shot from a neighboring hillside. When I got there, one of our hunters had just lit up one of those stinky old cigars. He was smiling proudly… "Bear's over there" he pointed.

Then, in a moment of bravery, he let out a southern war whoop and ran right up to the bruin. Leroy grabbed the animal by the ears and it came to life, letting out a blood curdling roar, tossing its head and Leroy. This was a lucky break for this foolish man because the bear lunged at a fallen log and tore a chunk out of it. Leroy lay several feet away and having no rifle close by, scurried back past me to the gun resting on his day pack. "Son of a b…; I'll kill ya this time," he yelled. He aimed and shot twice from ten yards distant and plowed dirt with both shots. The bear, thank goodness wasn't going anywhere because the first shot, the only shot that hit the animal was doing its job now and the bruin was succumbing.

It was over in moments and a visibly shaken Leroy was trying to find his mouth with a new cigar that shook violently in his fingers. "Damn critter could a killed us," he looked at me. "Did ya see what it did to that log, the son of a bi…! It's a good thing I can shoot under pressure!" I smiled and my boot brushed the two fresh dirt trenches his "after shots" had made.

"Yep, it's a good thing you can shoot alright," I grinned. We waited for one of my guides to arrive and dressed out the animal. I had an old work glove in my day pack and as we surgically removed the bruin's inwards, I decided to have a bit of fun, just to see how gullible some of these guys might be. I slid the work glove into the pile of intestines amidst the blood and stuff.

"Holy s… LeRoy," I exclaimed pulling the bloody glove from the bear's entrails. "You must've bagged one of the man eaters we have here! Look, he's still got someone's glove inside him." I winked at my guide and continued as brave LeRoy chewed nervously on his cigar. "This bear must have been the one that ate that hunter last spring. He was wearin' gloves just like these!"

"Wh… at…" LeRoy gulped and looked around the perimeter. "That's great, now let's get this guy loaded and check on the other guys. I didn't know we was huntin' man eaters, Ray. You could have told us!" He swallowed hard and bailed into the van leaving us outside to load the bruin. My guide and I exchanged smiles and giggled a bit.

Before the evening was over we had the last two bears down and headed homeward, smiling and happy. Now, in New Brunswick you cannot have a loaded gun in or on your motor vehicle and my "police/swat team" hunters had been given copies of our game laws along with specific instruction on the "do's and don'ts" of hunting. I always give our hunters a special seminar prior to starting a hunt and hopefully, most of what I say sinks in. When we arrived back at camp, I suggested that they all bring their weapons out and check them. "You mean unload them," Sarge asked innocently.

I smiled and replied "Yeh, right! Unload them!" To my astonishment, the sons of… guns… all had to unload their rifles which were already supposed to be empty. "What the heck is going on," I asked. "How long have these been loaded, guys?"

The Sarge stated that the guys always carried them fully loaded to their bear stands every day! "We didn't have our shotguns loaded when we were hunting grouse 'cause the book said we couldn't have a loaded gun in the vehicle when hunting but we figured there was no problem doing it for the bears. After all, we hunted bears using our rifles."

Once again, I shook my head and walked away. This was amazing and had a Forest Warden come along and asked to see the guns, both the hunters who had failed to comprehend their actions and even me, not knowing what they had done would have been in a world of trouble. That evening after the bruins had been skinned out and the meat quartered and on ice, the party of the year ensued at the lodge. 'Mr. Daniels', the swat team's good friend was joined by some guy called 'Captain Morgan' and a whole lot of 'Molson Canadians' and the fireside tales came fast and furious.

"Why, you should have seen me," LeRoy bragged. "If Ray hadn't stopped me, I would have wrestled that old man eater bear to the dirt and killed him with my "bare" hands…hah, hah! Get it…? "Bear" hands? Yep, ol' Ray here didn't want me to get my clothes dirty so I had to shoot that ugly son of a female dog twice more and all the while he was tryin' to tear up that log thinkin' it was me!"

Our sniper who finally had taken a huge bruin of probably sixty pounds soaking wet now interjected. "Yeh, I might a missed that big old bruin the other night but just try to hit one this size and him runnin' full tilt. Best shot I ever made!"

Somehow, I was willing to believe that. The evening grew late and the crew grew inarticulate so I wished them a good night and after several pats on the back from elated hunters, retreated to the quiet sanity of my house and warm bed. This encounter left me with a new outlook on life as we know it and some new perspectives on the guys in blue… or should I say black and, as we said our goodbyes the following day and they headed back home, I couldn't help but wonder what goes through the minds of those in desperate need when someone assesses the situation and asks the question…"Did someone call SWAT?"

Chapter 10
Buckhorn Vern

The very first time that I met Vern, who would eventually be affixed with the nickname "Buckhorn" Vern, I marveled at what the good Lord had created and… I reasoned that even the good Lord might be prone to making the odd mistake. He had arrived in camp, Vern… not the good Lord, on a rainy Sunday afternoon in deer season with a friend named Bob, a friend who seemed to follow him around like the small dog followed the big dog in that cartoon we used to watch when we were kids… Well alright… so I watched it at the age of forty-six. Still, if you can picture this huge man (Vern) with a tiny slip of a man (Bob) bouncing around at Vern's feet, eyes wide and tongue wagging constantly, then you get my drift. Now, back to ol' Buckhorn!

Vern, as I mentioned was a huge man, probably six foot six tall and a good 340 pounds plus soaking wet, a slight gut protruding under a massive barrel chest, long scraggily salt and pepper whiskers and mustache, three teeth spaced up top and one on the bottom jaw, puffy red cheeks and long, unkempt gray hair highlighted with various shades of black. His most distinguishing feature was his eyes or should I say one good eye. Well, it was as good as it was ever gonna get. He wore a patch over his left eye, a cat's eye marble glass eye but it was the right eye that really astounded me. That right eye didn't look straight out at the world. In fact, it veered off to the right a good twenty degrees and left me wondering when he talked, who he was addressing. Worse, when we checked out their guns at the rifle range, I was amazed and just a bit frightened when I saw how he had to hold the gun to look through the scope.

Little Bob, sort of a human descendent of Scrappy Doo I think, did make a reasonable shot on the target but when Vern stepped up to the bench and laid his head off to the left to use that one good eye, I gulped and breathed a sigh of relief that I was positioned well behind the bench. Ka-Bang! The shot echoed down range and a spout of dirt shot skyward off to the right of the target, possibly thirty yards away! I shook my head as Little Bob patted Vern on the shoulder. "Good shot Vern! What a shot! Dead center! That's one dead buck, buddy! One dead buck!" Little Bob danced around Vern as Vern swung that semi auto 7 mm Mag up again and let three more quick shots go, this time at arms length. I don't know where those shots eventually ended up but I later heard that Farmer Eatman lost two prize Holsteins that day in a pasture a half mile right of the firing range. Now, no one really knows what happened to those cows save to say that an autopsy revealed they had been shot!

I watched in disbelief as little Bob scampered to the targets and poked four holes in the center of Vern's with a bullet before bringing it to him. "What do ya think of that shootin', Vern? Great shootin', buddy! Yes, sir! Great shootin'!" I stood back with mouth agape, wondering if this huge one-eyed marvel of nature really thought that he could shoot straight. Needless to say, I was relieved when we arrived back in camp and the rifles were stowed away for the morning to come.

Supper on Sunday normally consists of freshly baked rolls and a big pot of chili and since we had only these two deer hunters in camp that week, I suspected that we'd be able to save on the grocery bill. Wrong! Both Vern and Little Bob could eat Vern's weight in

food and despite only having four teeth in his entire mouth, Vern could down just about anything… in a thoroughly disgusting manner. Vern was quite uncouth as well, having absolutely no table manners. As for his language, he was totally bilingual, spouting obscenities that would make a sailor blush. Between wiping his greasy hands on his or Bob's clothing, burping loudly and spitting particles of food in all directions, I ate little, very little that week!

Monday morning dawned gray and ominous with the occasional big Christmas flake of snow floating earthward. We hurriedly finished a big breakfast of bacon, sausage, eggs, home fries, pancakes, toast and coffee… well Little Bob and Buckhorn Vern did… I actually had trouble sitting there politely sipping and guarding my hot coffee against the "fallout" from Vern's mouth. "Gonna shoot me one of them big old hay racks this morning." Vern grinned that toothless grin, sort of drooling slightly as he made that statement. "Yeh Vern, Yeh! And I'm gonna shoot one too! Is it alright if I go with Vern… Ray? Is it?" Little Bob's eyes were wide with excited anticipation as he asked that question and he was almost panting like a puppy dog. I snowed on his idea. "No! I want to put you in another stand where we've been seeing some nice bucks."

Vern, recognizing the obvious disappointed look on his buddy's face interceded. 'Well, couldn't Bob come with me and "still hunt" that ridge area you showed me? He could "bird dog" for me… might even chase a big old brute right to me!" I sat there and could just picture it in my mind.

"Hmmm… Yeh, I guess you can do that. Just be careful not to shoot each other… and I'll hang close by as well." Little Bob jumped and pranced around the breakfast table and probably would have kissed or licked both Vern and I in his excitement save for me drawing away and Vern slapping him on the side of the head. "Calm down, ya dummy," Vern warned "or I won't let ya bird dog for me!"

As we drove the bumpy logging road, now covered with fresh white snow, I told them stories of past encounters with monster bucks, about the time I had spent most of the day tracking a huge buck only to find that it was an old matriarch doe with enormous feet, about the time two of our hunters called each other into shooting distance. But thankfully didn't shoot, and so on. The miles melted away and soon we were driving into the high country with a good four inches of snow down now.

Vern was chewing tobacco… or gumming it… and the juice was oozing down into his scraggly beard. Well, that explained the reddish brown tinted areas. And I never had to worry about him noticing when I stared because that toed out right eye was taking in all the landscape on the passenger side of the truck. It was difficult when I'd try to point out any landmark or reference point in front of or to the left side of the vehicle and there would be no use in depending on Little Bob to guide Vern. His eyes rarely left Vern's face. I felt sometimes like I was intruding on some pagan idol worship the way Little Bob stared at and worshipped Vern!

We deployed on a logging road at the top of a big beech and maple ridge in an area noted for feeding deer and big bucks. I think Vern took a compass reading although I'm not sure if he was eyeing the compass bearing or some trees off to his right. Anyhow, he and Little Bob loaded their rifles and headed off into the hardwood ridge. The snow had slowed by now so I felt sure that should anything go wrong, I would be able to find them before nightfall. I had a cup of coffee and a doughnut (should have been a policeman… the way I love doughnuts!) and I too, headed into the ridge.

I chose my path carefully, flanking the duo so as not to interfere with their hunting and I knew a shortcut to the brow of the ridge where I could watch a huge area and possibly even see them at times as they hunted. I gained a perch on the overhanging limbs of a big maple that had lodged in some beech trees, probably twenty feet up from the forest floor. It was a natural tree stand complete with limb floor and a limb seat so I was quite comfortable. Within the hour I could see the huge hunter orange blob, Vern plodding along in the snow a couple of hundred yards down on a plateau and some sixty or seventy yards distant, a smaller orange blob darting in and out of thickets, too quickly to be hunting himself. Suddenly, in some small spruce there was movement and a huge buck with a heavy massed rack bolted away from Little Bob. I sat up, quite alert now, with that old familiar adrenalin surge racing through my veins. The buck came across in front of Vern who immediately swung his head to the left away from the animal, supposedly zeroed his scope and fired, twice.

The buck staggered on the second shot as a limb fell from a beech tree and crashed onto the buck's back but Ol' Vern threw up his hands and did something that I had never seen done in all my years of guiding hunters. The buck lurched into a heavy spruce thicket, eight or ten feet tall with Vern crashing in right behind him. Seconds later, Vern came crashing back out yelling obscenities with the big buck applying horns to Vern's back side. Little Bob who had come tearing across the plateau to assist Vern had stopped dead in his tracks after seeing what was now happening. He turned and almost scampered up a big old maple tree, taking two limbs at a time! All the while, he was yelling loudly… "Run Vern! Run! Do you need help Vern? I'll help ya, buddy," but from where I sat, he didn't seem to be moving to help Vern!

Vern swatted several times at the buck, each time it applied the horns but Vern continued to try to do the four minute mile, not an easy feat for someone of his size and build. Finally, one of his wild swings with gun in hand connected with the buck's head and the beast dropped in its tracks. Vern stopped running and turned to see the buck lying very still in the snow. He looked all around to make sure no one was watching and hurried back to the still animal. "I got him, Bob! I got him… little buddy!" Bob was still climbing towards the top of the tree when he heard the news and I was laughing so hard I almost took a double gainer out of my perch.

It took me ten minutes to regain my composure and arrive on the scene where "Buckhorn Vern", now his official name stood proudly over a dressed out twelve-pointer. Not letting on that I had witnessed the entire thing, I asked if it took only one shot or the two that I had heard. "Nahww… he went down with the first shot, Ray, right in a heap… so I fired the second shot to signal Little Bob… ain't that right Little Bob?" Little Bob seemed to be a bit uncomfortable with the lying but Ol' Buckhorn was his hero and besides, he was so busy climbing that tree, he hadn't seen what actually brought the buck down finally.

We drove back to camp with Vern's prize and skinned out the animal. We found no bullet holes anywhere; just a bruise from the falling tree limb that had hit the buck's back and rump. Still, we took pictures and capped the trophy for mounting. Little Bob hunted very little the remainder of the week, preferring to ride with Ol' Buckhorn and I as we searched for grouse. This in itself afforded much amusement for me as "Vernie" fired at twenty plus grouse and cut limbs off in nearby trees, shot one crow by mistake and peppered my truck with birdshot as we returned from a walk and flushed a bird near the truck. It was a memorable hunt, there is no question and taught me some valuable lessons as well. A well-aimed blow with your rifle butt can stop and indeed kill a charging white tail buck. If you can put up with the patronizing and lap dogging, friends like Little Bob may actually prove useful and finally I have to say this. Buckhorn Vern is the only hunter, who has ever posed for a photo with a trophy buck, yet appears to be looking off into the bushes and grinning! I guess we all have different views on life… I know Ol' Buckhorn sure does!

Chapter 11
Griz McCoy and
the Black Ridge Bear!

As the huge bruin sniffed curiously, Manzer sat very still, trying to hold both his breath and his heart from beating its way out of his chest! His rifle lay several yards away at the foot of the treestand… several yards from where he now squatted. Only the occasional distant bird's song could be heard in the deafening silence, that and the snuff-snuff-snuffing of a bear that was growing more agitated at this camouflaged lump of whatever that huddled between him and the bear bait. The neck and back hairs stood now and the bear moved closer, shaking his head from side to side, his slavering jaws pop-popping as he approached. He smelled honey but he also smelled the overpowering body odor of one, Griz McCoy, bear hunter extraordinaire, fearless predator of the dark forest, the "drop me anywhere and don't come back for me for a week" hunter who now shook like a leaf in a hurricane. The moment of truth was at hand, and Griz could feel the hot foul breath on his neck. He turned ever so slowly to face his nemesis with slavering gaping maw just as the bear's red rag of a tongue appeared and licked…

Okay, folks, I know… you want to know what happened to our hunter but let's go back to the day this spring bear hunter arrived at camp. It was a clear morning with that big golden sun sitting in an azure sky, surveying puffy marshmallow clouds as they drifted by (what do you think of that descriptive narrative?). I was doing a chore that I don't particularly enjoy during springtime; mowing an acre of lawn. As I stopped to mop my brow, I could hear a vehicle racing along the valley road towards me. Squealing, howling tires, a roaring engine and finally screeching brakes as the 4x4 SUV came to rest a hundred yards past our "Welcome to Malarkey Cabin" sign. The driver leaned out the window and looked back, then turned his SUV right in the middle of the road and came back. The license plate coupled with the first Advantage Camouflage SUV I have ever seen told me that this was one of our bear hunters.

"How the heck do you guys drive the speed limit up here in Canada," he grinned. "I've been tryin' but the best I could get out of this old Ford was 85 miles an hour, tops and the speed limit signs say 100! You guys must be crazy! By the way, I'm Manzer McCoy… my friends all call me "Griz" and you can too. Been huntin' bear most of my life… love the outdoors as you can see…" And with that he stepped from the rolling hunting blind. I surveyed this gentleman much the same as I do all hunters and those who would be hunters when they arrive.

"Griz" was mid-forties but looked to be in late fifties and had obviously abused himself in his early years. He was shallow cheeked with sunken eyes, a scruffy beard which many outdoorsmen seem to possess, shaggy uncombed hair that almost rested on his narrow shoulders, lean of frame and he walked with a stoop and a shuffle. His apparel was well worn and accentuated with tree moss interwoven in both a rattlesnake skin belt and in and out through his camo floppy hat ammunition holder. He wore high-topped hunting boots that had seen lots of wear and he proudly displayed a Maine Master Guide patch on the sleeve of his Camouflage shirt. He looked like he could guide me, a real honest to goodness woodsman… and he smelled it. Whew! The body odor was almost overpowering!

I led him to the lodge and helped carry some two hundred pounds of outdoor gear inside. He had almost every outdoor product I had ever seen and this further impressed this ol' country boy from New Brunswick. Breakfast the first morning came and went without incident although the other hunters swarmed my end of the dining table and left "Griz" by himself at the other end. Several hunters commented about just how important they felt personal hygiene is but that seemed to soar over Griz's head. He did much of his eating with his filthy hands and wiped the excess food and grease on his pants or shirt to the dismay of the rest of our crew and me!

The first afternoon saw the other hunters fire up their trucks and head to their bear baits and stands but old Griz couldn't get his SUV to start. As the time ticked away, I reluctantly grabbed his gear and drove him to his location in my truck. I asked if he'd allow me to cover scent him but he declined. "Ya know, Ray, I never even take a shower when I'm on a hunt! No siree, man! I don't want them bears smellin' no fancy soaps or perfumes! No way! I want to be totally natural!" I tried to explain to him that "totally natural" simply meant matching your hunting surroundings, using various cover scents or odor neutralizer or rubbing your hunting clothes and gear with spruce or fir or cedar boughs. That didn't sink in either.

The first afternoon and evening went fast. Two of our hunters saw bears and one bagged his very first. One of my guides helped him with that one while I drove up to check on Griz. There was still an hour before dark but he had already vacated his tree stand and stood on the side of the road, leaning on the barrel of his gun. "Good evening sir," I grinned as I rolled up beside him. He looked over at me and nodded. "Did you see anything," I asked.

"Not a thing," came the reply. I proceeded to ask why he was out from his bait site so early given the fact that prime hunting time is usually the last hour of the day. "Got tired of seein' nothing, so I checked out the bait in the barrel. My outfitter has got some prime stuff in there! Good gravy, a couple of those donuts weren't hurt at all so I ate 'em. Ain't gonna give good food to the bears, ya know!" He wiped his hands on his camo pants and walked over to lean up against my truck.

"Do you know Ray Dillon," he asked without blinking an eye or grinning. I smiled and replied that I did know the gentleman. "Great outfitter and guide, he is," I grinned. Griz shook his head and shot back that he didn't know me that well as yet but that I seemed to be a pretty decent fellow. It was about this time that I started to wonder if he recognized me or the truck. "Can I give you a lift," I asked. "Naw… I better wait for Ray. He'll be along soon." I sat there in disbelief. Here was a guy who had actually believed that our road speed signs were in miles per hour rather than kilometers per hour. He thought that smelling natural for the hunt meant not bathing and now, he didn't recognize his guide or the guide's vehicle that had delivered him to this site, just hours ago. "He must have did a lot of drugs back in the sixties and seventies," I thought.

"Well, come on Griz. I'll take you back to camp," I laughed. He started to protest but I quickly explained that I not only knew Ray but also was in fact, him! Griz stepped back and looked at both me and my truck with a puzzled look on his face. "Well, where'd you get this truck," he asked. "It's the same one that brought you out here," I laughed again. He got in and deposited his gear in the back seat and turned with, "Are you sure this is the same truck? Well, did you paint it this afternoon?" I just shook my head and drove.

The week proceeded without similar incidents. Griz had some strange ideas about bear hunting though and after all our other hunters had scored or missed their bears and he hadn't even seen one,

I took him aside and humbly asked if he had ever taken a bear. "Oh, I've hunted 'em for years," he replied but I found that quite evasive. "Well, have you ever taken one?" "No!" "Ever seen one while on stand?" "No… so what're you getting at?" "Maybe we should try some honey… a honey burn," I suggested, "and we have got to cover scent you." He insisted that he would do the honey burn and apply cover scent himself and didn't want or need my help. "I did graduate from taking a Master Guide's course in Maine, ya know!" I left him on that fateful afternoon with all the ingredients for… what I thought would be a good evening hunt! All he needed to do was follow my directions.

After I had gone, ol' Griz decided that he knew more than his flustered old Canadian guide. Instead of using that cover scent and doing a honey burn, he smeared himself with honey and promptly left his rifle to venture off towards the bait to see what goodies I had in that barrel. Half way there, he caught a glimpse of the bear and not knowing what else to do, he squatted down believing that his camouflage would hide him from the bruin. Now he was between the hungry bear and a meal. Well, the old "bring 'em to me and I'll tear him apart with my bare hands" was now forgotten in the intensity of the moment.

I was witness to what happened next since I had found Griz's flashlight in my truck and figured he might need it if he stayed on the stand until dark. I had approached the bait site quietly and couldn't believe the predicament he was in at this moment. The big boar bear took a big lick of Griz's gaunt face and snorted. I swear that the bear actually spat as he wheeled around to run. In all my years of guiding, I have never seen a bear have such a look of disgust on his face nor have I ever seen a fearless bear hunter jump up, rush headlong into the tree that housed his stand and collapse next to his rifle.

I carried the old Master Guide to my truck, keeping my head

turned away so as not to smell him. We revived him back at the lodge and after I told him that I had found him at the base of the tree, unconscious, he quickly spun a lie that Mark Twain would have been proud of. "Ya see, I had come down from my tree just at dark and this monster bear was awaitin' for me. We fought and rolled around and I guess I must have rolled through that honey burn cause I got honey all over me. Well, I hit that bear just as he hit me and you guys won't believe it but I run him off before I fell unconscious." The other bear hunters would have patted his shoulder but opted instead to simply offer their praise of his heroic efforts from a safe smelling distance. As for me, I smiled! "You are a "Master", Griz," I mumbled to myself. I shook my head… But you'd a made a better politician than a bear hunter!

Chapter 12
Mad Munchey -
Splitting Hairs?

Monty Muncher came to us from one of the States that lies south of the Mason-Dixon Line. It was a cold, rainy Sunday morning in November when Monty's big new Silverado 4x4 roared into our driveway towing a long trailer loaded down with boxes of hunting gear, a twenty cubic foot freezer and a camouflaged All Terrain Vehicle, known as a "Quad", a "Wheeler" or to many of us, as an "ATV." He drove right up to our house in this huge, menacing, tinted window beast and I half expected a mountain man to disembark, complete with heavy beard, rippling muscles and a barrel chest.

Instead and to my surprise, out jumped a little fellow, not much more than four feet tall and Smurf- like in stature. He did have a heavy, ragged beard and he wore all the camouflage clothing that hunters wear and as he strode toward our house with chest puffed, shoulders squared and arms extended like a miniature wrestler, I imagined that somewhere, some little girl was missing her Gremlin doll. This was short lived as he bounced up on the porch deck where I stood. "Y'all must be Ray," he grinned. I reached for the tiny extended hand and felt the short stubby fingers close in a firm handshake. "Damn if it ain't a long drive comin' up here," he offered. "My butt has been clean pushed up to ma ears sittin' so long." I opened our dining hall door and motioned for him to come inside.

Now I could attempt to write this account down using spelling in the dialogue that would compliment his heavy southern accent but it would be difficult for me to write and possibly quite difficult for you to understand so I will keep it simple and ask that you picture this little man as having been one of the actors in *Gone With the Wind* or some other southern movie. With his long red hair, his scraggly beard and wooly eyebrows perched on a sharp, weathered face, he could have starred as the Leprechaun in the movie of the same name. He only needed to wear the Irish green and the pointed toe shoes. His deep blue eyes stared fiercely under the shaggy brows but his little pot belly shook every time he laughed heartily and so you felt at ease with him, despite the stare.

"How's the deer huntin' been," he queried as he admired the trophy buck heads on our walls.

"We've taken half dozen good ones, several smaller ones and two Boone and Crockett monsters so far, Monty."

He swung his gaze from the fireplace and the thirteen pointer hanging above it and settled on me. "Y'all call me Munchey now, hear? All my friends call me Munchey. I don't know why but that nickname has stuck since I was just a small boy." With that statement, he swung about once more to admire the live bear and wild turkey mounts in the corners of the room and he stopped and stared up with mouth agape in front of the huge bull moose head on a side wall. "My gawd, it's damn near a dinosaur," he gasped. "I ain't never seen anything that big… and they walk these woods we will be huntin'?"

I don't know if it was Munchey's diminutive appearance or the moose's huge size but suddenly that old bull did look like a prehistoric monster and I was so proud. Anyhow, I got Munchey's gear stowed away in the lodge before I noticed something even more bizarre. At first, I thought I might be mistaken but no, there it was again. Munchey was carrying on a conversation… with himself. Now I may have told you of other hunters we have had in camp who have done so as well but Munchey would actually get into arguments with himself… animated arguments that became so fierce, I half believed he would attack himself physically. It would prove to be an interesting week for deer hunting.

On Monday morning, the rain had changed to a Christmas snow with big wet flakes that drifted down to cover the earth in a soft white blanket. It was the kind of snow that gets deer hunters excited… the kind of snow that stirs big old bucks to move about in the deep woods and along the forest edges, leaving fresh tracks for any and all to see. Munchey was driving along behind me with his own 4x4 truck, still towing the ATV on the trailer with the freezer still sitting at the front, ahead of the Wheeler. I had suggested that he unhitch the trailer and load the bike (ATV) onto the pickup bed of his truck if he wished to take it along and there really wouldn't be a need to drag along the freezer until he had downed, skinned out and processed his deer.

That idea did appeal to Munchey initially but his other personality soon emerged right there in front of me and the dialogue went like this. Munchey… the Munchey I met first when he arrived in camp, agreed that we should unload the bike and freezer and unhook the trailer. As he had walked to the trailer hitch to undo it, suddenly his head jerked back and he stood upright, thumping himself in the forehead. "What are you doin' stupid? You'll have to go through this all again when you leave here." I thought he was talking with me and so I moved closer behind him to hear so I could respond.

He responded himself in the original persona. "It don't make sense to tow the trailer and bike out into the huntin' country like Ray said. Let's unhook it." He bent over to do so but once again, his head jerked back and he stood up "No, no, no! Let's do it like I said. Leave the damned trailer alone stupid! It won't hurt to take it out there and back and it will save us time and effort when we leave!" Personality number two made the final decision right in front of me, quite oblivious to the fact that I was there and so on the first morning of the hunt, I watched his miniature wagon train pull up the rear.

We were going to hunt the high country and he was the only hunter in camp so I could provide him or in his case… "them" my personal attention. I couldn't help but admire that new Chevy 4x4. My old clunker Chevy was still going but you can't beat those new smooth purring trucks for performance and comfort. Still, my old Chevy's truck bed had seen more deer and bear and moose trophies than most trucks will ever see and for that I was thankful. We stopped at the mouth of a side road that jutted off into heavy woods on one side and big two year old clear cuts on the other. Munchey got out chewing on some crunchy candies and I couldn't help but notice a slight dribble of saliva winding its way through that tangle of beard. "You're drooling on your beard, Munchey," I grinned. "The deer won't like that." It was meant to alert him to his dribbling and to do so with a tiny bit of humour.

Instead, he looked up at me fiercely (remember that Munchey was barely four feet tall and I looked like the Friendly Giant along side him) and cleared his throat. "You jest show me whar them critters is. They won't know I'm droolin' when I bang 'em down." I apologize, folks but I had to give you an example of that southern slang. Translated… "Please show me where those deer are and I believe I can harvest one prior to them noticing any salivation problems that may have occurred." Now, which version do you like?

I started to have concerns with Munchey and his hunting abilities when he brought out his Day Pack and a large assortment of candies and potato chips fell out onto the ground. These were followed by two bottles of "pop" or "sodas", depending on where you hail from, and by a large bag of peanuts in the shell. All such treats were either wrapped in noisy cellophane or plastic wrap, or encased in a noisy shell. There was a bottle of Vicks VapoRub, great to ease cold symptoms or un-stuff a nose but a bad scent to be wearing or using in the deer woods. Munchey stooped to stuff the goods back in his Day Pack and proceeded to zip it closed this time. As I stated, I did have some concerns about Munchey's hunting abilities but it was what happened next that really concerned me.

I had outlined the area on a map and was proceeding to describe the lay of the land for him when all of a sudden, he blurted out, "I think we should hunt the deep woods today."

"Well, you can hunt where you want to. I've scouted these areas and there are lots of deer here and some big bucks," I responded. The problem was that Munchey wasn't directing his conversation to me.

At this point, Munchey One (we probably should call his personalities Munchey One and Munchey Two for clarity) responded totally ignoring me. "Well, I think we should hunt up back of these clear cuts or at least on the edge of one."

"No, I want to hunt the big woods!" Each time he'd change personalities, he would look to the left or right and actually change facial expressions and voice depth. I have to admit, I was beginning to have some misgivings about this entire hunt.

Munchey One seemed to be the nicer of the two personalities and would acknowledge my presence and advice. On the other hand, Munchey Two appeared to be the dominant personality and would often raise his voice, grimace menacingly and totally ignore anything I said. He wouldn't even acknowledge that I was there. I wasn't real happy when Munchey Two carried the rifle but he seemed more interested in bossing Munchey One around than anything else. It was almost like watching some weird comedy as Munchey One and Two discussed where they were going to hunt. In fact, Munchey One liked to stand hunt while Munchey Two wanted to stalk. I grinned as I stood behind the pair of personalities embodied in the one hunter and wondered if this meant they both had shared the cost of the hunting trip. "Ain't nobody going to believe this one anyway," I thought.

Eventually, Munchey Two won the discussion and I left the hunter stalking down the old side logging road in the snow. He was headed towards the heavy woods to the East and I thought, probably a good choice in this kind of weather. The deer would be moving about in the heavy woods and Munchey might get a crack. This was early morning but still quite dark due to the overcast skies and snowfall. Not wishing to leave the area for any length of time, I drove my old truck up the road a mile or so and turned it so I could peer back down where Munchey had parked his truck and trailer. Snow fell quite heavily for several hours and despite listening patiently, I heard no shots. All I could hear was the heavy hiss of falling snow.

Throughout the morning, I watched numerous deer walk across the old logging road, heading away from the wooded area Munchey was hunting. On several occasions, I saw bucks with big racks cross and all stopped and looked back in the direction they came from. I was curious as to just what might be transpiring so I drove back down, parked near Munchey's caravan and walked down the old road. I hadn't gone a couple of hundred yards when I heard elevated voices arguing. It was a heated argument and I sincerely wondered if Munchey had encountered another hunter by chance and had somehow become engaged in a verbal altercation.

I hurried around the bend in the road only to find Munchey

standing there firmly gripping his coat by the neck as though he feared losing it in a windstorm. "Listen, ya son of a…" he growled. "I told ya I ain't gonna walk anymore. My legs are hurtin'." He sort of brushed his hands away from the coat in much the same manner as someone would if they were being choked by an opponent.

"Well go back to the truck, ya sissy. I'm gonna skirt that clear cut over there so you do whatever you want." As I mentioned, this entire conversation was loud and to me quite humorous but what made it even more so was the fact that a nice eight-point buck came out to cross the road just then, not more than forty yards distant. The animal stopped and swung the heavy racked head in our direction.

"Munchey, there's your buck. Take him," I whispered excitedly.

As I live and breathe, what happened next came right out of the pages of *Ripley's Believe it or Not!* Munchey raised the rifle and aimed at the big buck but before he could shoot, he jerked the rifle downward. "It's my buck! I'm shootin' it," he hissed.

"No way! I saw it first, didn't I Ray?" came the rebuttal. I stepped back out of harm's way and I might add, quite concerned as the two personalities argued back and forth. The buck had stepped up onto the road and crossed it by now, peering quite curiously at the two… or three of us depending on how you look at it, standing forty yards distant with at least two of our party in heated argument. I cleared my throat and hesitantly touched Munchey's shoulder.

"The buck is gettin' away. Shoot it Munchey," I implored. One of the pair and I'm not sure which one, swung around and gave me a piercing look. I backed off. The rifle rose once again and then lowered as quickly. The buck strode into the woods with a parting look over his shoulder and I stood there shaking my head. Munchey One and Munchey Two hadn't noticed that the buck had gone as the "joined

in the body" personalities continued to argue. I turned and walked briskly to the truck.

I was genuinely concerned at this point. I had never dealt with such a man or should I say "men." Tomorrow would be "stand day" and I would insist on that.

I don't know when Munchey finished the argument with his alter ego but I do know that he drove back to camp in the falling snow that evening without a deer. My sleep that night was fitful as I tossed and turned and thought of this strange Leprechaun hunter. It seemed like I had just closed my eyes when the radio alarm sounded and some announcer blared "Good morning New Brunswick. It's time to rise and shine here in the picture province and we've got a fresh blanket of snow for you this morning." I rolled over and glared at the clock radio. I was tired but it was time to get up and have breakfast, according to all those outdoor magazines I had read as a kid.

If you want to be a successful deer hunter, then you must be up several hours before daylight. You then devour a hearty breakfast containing so many calories and so much fat and cholesterol that you'll be lucky to get to the deer woods before the sun comes up and really lucky if you get there without having a heart attack or stroke. Then you sit on a stand or in a ground blind and freeze you're a.... . Then, when the sun finally does come up and a deer finally does get up and come by around nine o'clock, you'll be so cold and stiff and frozen; you won't be able to shoot anyhow. Magazines that give you such advice do serve a good purpose. You can use them to start a fire and thaw out!

Anyhow, Ol' Munchey grabbed his back pack, donned some heavy hunting clothes and away we went in pitch black darkness. This morning, since he and his alter ego were the only two hunters in camp, I drove them. Being in the same body, they only took up room for one person in my old Chevy Silverado extended cab pickup.

We drove out into the high country with a six inch blanket of fresh snow covering the woodlands and I was thankful for the snow tires and my truck's four wheel drive system. Munchey may have found and actually taken his medication that morning because he sat quietly, mumbling and nodding only occasionally. Within a half hour, we had arrived where he was to hunt that day.

"Here Ray, carry my pack please," he grinned.

A quick snap of his neck and he turned to growl, "Carry the pack, yourself." Once again a small argument ensued and I stood by listening. Finally, Munchey One got his way and I carried the day pack for the little gnome while he, they, carried the gun and case. Daylight was now fast approaching so we hurried along to a ground blind I had constructed. We set up a portable chair which both Munchey's seemed to like and I cover scented him or them, and left the area.

As I departed, I whispered that I would be returning around ten o'clock to rattle and call. "Just sit quiet and watch," I urged. "The deer come down that trail to the brook and it's only forty yards from this blind so you must sit quietly."

"Don't worry, I won't make a sound," Munchey smiled. "Me neither," came another reply as that red head turned.

It was a quiet morning in the deer woods and had turned cold despite the new snow. The air seemed to carry every crunchy foot-step as I walked back to the truck. I was very confident that Munchey would get his shot this morning… provided the other Munchey living in that body would let him. I left the area and drove a half mile or so away and then disembarked to wait and listen for shots. Several hours, four donuts and two steaming cups of coffee later, I decided to go back to the blind and do some calling and rattling. I couldn't understand why Munchey hadn't fired a shot by now. Deer regularly traveled down that trail past the blind and to the stream bank for a drink but apparently none had thus far this morning. I stopped the truck and walked slowly down the trail to the blind. My steps were crunching in the snow but I stopped several times because I heard other noises… loud noises coming from the blind area.

I moved within twenty yards behind the blind and heard a crunch-crunch sound inside the blind, followed by loud munching and a burp. There was the distinct sound of crinkling plastic paper and I could hear every time a peanut was shelled. Then there was the mumbling… and sharp whispers as the head jerked from one side to the other. Well, with all that blasted noise, why the heck were they… or him whispering? I looked beyond at the deer trail and saw absolutely no deer tracks when there should have been at least a hundred or so. I stood there and shook my head in disgust.

It was bad enough that I had two hunters in one body and only one of them had paid for the hunt. It was even worse that when one had an opportunity the day before to shoot a nice buck, his other self wouldn't let him, opting to bag the buck instead. Now, I had a noisy munching machine sitting in one of my favorite, productive ground blinds drowning out any and all other woodland sounds. I walked on up to the blind and stood off to one side. Munchey never missed a beat. He was eating so loudly that he didn't hear me walk up and still munching as I clattered the rattling antlers together. He still didn't acknowledge me. I rattled for several minutes and watched him eat. It was candy, peanut, candy, peanut, drink of juice, and back to peanut. Shoot! I could see why he was nicknamed "Munchey."

Now, I have seen many things in my life as a guide but what I witnessed in the next few seconds will go down in history as one of the most memorable, if not unbelievable. I know you are gonna shake your heads and think this old Irishman is stringing some Malarkey but I have to tell you, anyhow. I stopped rattling those antlers and started to walk over to the blind. At that moment, Munchey looked my way, crunching on a mouthful of peanuts and candy. On my right, a huge buck stepped from the underbrush. Munchey raised the rifle and I hit the ground, partly because I was kind of in the line of fire and partly because I didn't know what would happen next. Ka-Bang! Ka-Bang!

The buck never missed a step. He walked right down the trail, nose to the ground and into the bushes twenty yards distant. Munchey jumped up and charged down the trail, gun raised and short little legs pounding the ground. He charged into the bushes as I picked myself up. Ka-Bang! Ka-Bang! "Why you son of a b…! You shot my buck!"

"No, he's mine!"

"No, he's… shoot… he ain't dead." With that I stood and watched Munchey come running from the underbrush with an angry monster buck in pursuit.

"Shoot him! Shoot him, you fool!" The head jerked to the other side, scraggly beard and long hair flapping in the breeze as Munchey came tearing by the ground blind and me.

"No, he's your buck! You shoot him." The buck had given up on the chase and bounded off down the trail as Munchey One and Two raced for the road and the safety of the truck. I walked back to the truck that morning on crunchy snow, shaking my head. I thought what a great story this would make… a Leprechaun with twin personalities and both of them like to hunt and argue with each other… and then I shook my head again… no… who the hell would believe it?

Chapter 13
Foolish Questions

Being a hunting guide for more than thirty years has brought me face to face with some real characters, characters who posed some unbelievable questions and in this chapter, I would like to share some of these with you. I'm sure that you've heard that the only foolish question is the one that goes unasked? Well, that's only partially true. There are some people who will ask a question to impress you or their friends and there are people who must have some other reason for asking, besides seeking an answer, possibly to fake interest in what you are about.

There are some crazy, really crazy questions I have been asked but until you can qualify them with the situation, you might not think they are out of line. They do demonstrate that an experienced hunter cannot assume that a novice hunter will even know the basics of hunting or being out in the woods. A common sense reaction for the untrained hunter, when faced with the moment of truth, may be elusive and hence, strange questions arise. Let's look at some.

"Which way is north?" The deer hunter was standing in the big woods of New Brunswick on the first morning of his deer hunt. The guy was holding his new compass vertically with the price tag still dangling! What's wrong with this picture? Well, in the first place, we should never expect to take a quick orienteering course when we know absolutely nothing about a compass or direction or how to even read a compass. Simply purchasing one of those little hand held "needle-y" things ain't gonna get you anywhere you wish to go, and what is really more ironic is the money that some nimrods spend on one. I've seen guys standing around in a group comparing their compasses and what they spent for them, yet not having the faintest idea how to use one! That's right guys! The big woods of New Brunswick is definitely not the place to be learning about a compass. And here's another tip. You can own a Porsche or a Volkswagen but neither one is worth a hoot unless you can drive!

One of my fondest memories stems from just such an incident as this. We had hunters in camp from a hunting club. They all arrived with brand new gear, complete with dangling price tags but assured me they were seasoned veterans in the woods. "Yah, we been huntin' the big woods for fifteen years," the club president confided, "and we come here for your big bucks. Got one of them new GPS (Global Positioning System) units and there ain't no woods I won't go in." I was pleased to hear this despite my doubts so before first light on opening morning of deer season, tags had been removed from new Gore-Tex clothing, instructions given as to what I expected of the hunters and off we drove to the deer woods. When we arrived at a small block of wilderness approximately three square miles or so, the remarks began to flow as well as the questions.

"Damn, this is big woods," one hunter remarked… "and thick stuff too! You better take one of those GPS readings, Mac," which Mac attempted to do before we disembarked. I suggested that he wait till he was outside the van but then found that it really wouldn't make a bit of difference since Mac had never used a GPS unit in his life. To make matters worse, I even had to show him how to install the batteries. One of the other hunters had brought out a brand new expensive compass and was busy turning with the spinning compass needle. "I can't catch up to the bloody thing," he remarked to the other two guys who were busy doing their own spin jobs. "Guys, guys," I interrupted, "maybe I should take you all in and hunt you on stands." "Hell no," the club president spoke up. "All we need is some direction and advice and we'll be alright. These woods don't scare us!" I fought the urge to grin as two of the hunters still pirouetted around trying to catch the magnetic needle that struggled in vain to show them north on their compasses. (They were only slightly ahead of the guy holding his compass vertically, looking for the northern sky.)

I attempted to explain waypoints and icons to the chief with the GPS but finally gave up. I opted instead to give everyone a crash compass course and nervously watched as these naïve "hunters" plunged head first into the unknown! It kept me and two guides busy the entire week retrieving these boys and re-instructing them on compass reading. Despite the fact that the President had no inkling of how to operate a GPS unit, he still insisted on hauling it out of his pack periodically to fiddle with for lengthy periods of time. Needless to say, the guys bagged no deer although they scared the hell out of quite a few as they staggered about, constantly searching for "north" on the compass.

Another often asked question from hunters usually went like this. "Which direction will the bear, moose or deer come from?" Innocent enough, I suppose but this question still amazes me. The fact that every animal has his or her own personality and motivations, suspicions and reactions needs to be considered here. The idea that the guide will know where the animal will come from suggests that the guide is much more than a guide, perhaps a god. This takes me back to a young hunter who came to us seeking black bear one spring. He was an eager novice full of questions. He had taken no time to research the animal he was hunting. Furthermore, he had never actually seen a bear in the wild. I spent considerable time coaching him, informing him of what to look for, the possible scenarios he might expect and what to shoot or decline. In New Brunswick, it is illegal to take a sow bear with cubs and so we dwell on this point with our hunters to insure that no accidents occur.

I felt that Tommy was basically ready to hunt when I led him to the ground blind and "scented" him up with an attractant cover scent. Now as the moment of truth arrived, Tommy was becoming a bit nervous. I reassured him calmly directing his attention to the bait site and his field of fire. "Make sure you take him in the brisket if he's facing you, or mid-way in the shoulder if he's broadside," I whispered. As I turned to walk away, he hissed, "Which way will he come in?" I swung about and pointed towards the southwest corner of the opening. "He'll come in right there at 8:30 p.m. on the dot so you be ready!" I grinned and shook my head but Tommy wasn't amused. He

nodded and settled in, glancing at his watch that now showed 4 o'clock. That night, when by some miracle of coincidence a 250-pound boar came in to the bait from the southwest corner at precisely 8:30 p.m., Tommy thought I was the "bear god" and all my laughing explanations that this had been a joke made no difference to him!

"When should I shoot?" should be a valid question but it can sometimes lead to unbelievable events happening. I recall a bear hunter who asked me that question as he and some buddies sat at the dinner table. I looked at him and suggested that I thought the best time to bag a bear would be when he was preoccupied with eating, in effect, when his head was in the bucket. That simple answer cost the hunter a huge boar and taught me a valuable lesson. It was a hot sweltering afternoon in early June (spring bear season in New Brunswick runs from mid-April until the end of June) and our hunters huddled in tree stands or ground blinds wrapped in confining bug suits with salty perspiration trickling down their faces and burning their eyes. Swarms of biting insects hovered about them in clouds and conditions were nasty but this was definitely a bear-killing afternoon!

My guides and I were doing "burns" on each client bait site, a process where you actually boil honey and molasses in a tin can over a small portable stove. The heated molecules rise into the air currents and will attract bruins (another name for bears) from considerable distances. My hunter, Ed sat stone faced and quiet watching the lush green forest when he noticed a large black patch that didn't seem to fit in. He came to full attention when that patch moved and stepped into the opening to reveal a massive black bear. It stopped a mere forty yards from the bait and surveyed the burn in progress, sniffing loudly and testing the air currents suspiciously. It offered a motionless target at forty yards and Ed had zeroed his scope on the brisket but didn't shoot. For a full five minutes, he rested his gun on the shooting cross bar in that blind while the bear stood there. Finally the bear grew nervous and turned to leave but stopped once more broadside to look. Ed centered his cross hairs on the big shoulder but didn't shoot either. Then, with a quick backward glance, the bear faded into the surrounding foliage and was gone.

When Ed told me the blow-by-blow story, I was almost dumb-founded. "Why didn't you take him," I asked unbelievably. He responded in a very serious tone. "You told me not to shoot unless his head was in the bucket." I was dumbfounded. With an amused look, I quickly elaborated on my original answer to his question. It was too late for that particular situation but he did get a nice bear before the week ended and I learned to make myself perfectly clear when I responded to a question, no matter how foolish or simple I might think it to be! A similar situation arose when a client innocently asked where his bear would show up. At first, I looked at him in disbelief but realizing that he wasn't just joking, I shrugged.

Another amusing question brought this response. "Ah... I don't really know Matt. They can come in from any direction, even from behind your blind." "Well... Where do you think that bear will be when I see him," he persisted looking nervously over his right shoulder at the heavily wooded path we had just come in on. I shook my head and checked the late afternoon breeze as it scattered smoke from our honey burn into the woods in front of our hunter. "He'll probably come in down wind to the right or left of the bait," I reassured him. "At any rate, I'd be very surprised if he came in behind you cause he'd be traveling with the wind instead of into it so he'll probably be right at the bait when you first see him. So calm down and rest easy and tonight may be your night! Take a big one!"

With that parting statement and a slap on his shoulder, I moved off into the lush greenery of the spring woodlands. A couple of my guides had been baiting other sites and placing hunters on stands or in blinds and were now waiting for me at a logging road intersection. "Gonna be a good night for bears," John offered. "I did my bear dance this afternoon so we'll get bears tonight!" (John spent a lifetime in the military where he proceeded to learn absolutely nothing. Furthermore, he had banged his head against tank roofs on too many occasions! He was a good friend and the camp clown and we all loved him and we knew that when John did a bear dance… like the mythical rain dance, things would happen… not necessarily involving bears… but we might get rain or something!) I left John and my other guide, Dave to check on some other baits.

It was a bit after seven o'clock when I got back to Matt's blind site. As I drove up, he was standing nervously by the roadside, smoking a cigarette, visibly shaken. He rushed over even before I got the door open and blurted "Damned bear came in right behind me! Right fair behind my blind! Scared the shi… out of me!"

"Whoa Matt. Calm down! Did you get him?"

"Get him? Get him? Hell, I was so surprised! Ya… you, you said he'd come in from behind the bait! You said he wouldn't come in behind me," he was sputtering, half angry, half scared and breathing raggedly.

"Matt, I have no way of knowing what a wild animal will do or not do and I can't control where he goes. Now, take a deep breath and calm down. What happened that got you so worked up?"

The hunter in question hadn't expected a bear to come in from behind, basing that belief on his questions and my response. The bear had done nothing wrong. It had simply defied logic and approached with its rump in the wind instead of its nose. When it ambled on by the blind, Matt had become startled, jumped up, said a few choice words and vacated his blind for the inviting bright light of the logging road opening, some sixty yards along the path behind the blind. The bear also became startled and beat a hasty retreat right on past the bait site as evidenced by the torn up earth and trail. I did eventually calm Matt down and convinced him to take a tree stand in the open overlooking a clear-cut area. Here, he felt reasonably comfortable and before the week was through, his 375 H&H Big Bore (an over powered elephant gun for bear hunting – sort of like swatting a fly with a sledge hammer) claimed a good one hundred and sixty pound young dry sow.

Foolish questions? I believe that no question is foolish or stupid unless we intend it that way. Unbelievable questions, ridiculous when asked out loud may just be a cry for reassurance or attention. And that old adage that the only stupid question is the one not asked? That is just the response of a kindly outfitter or guide to reassure the hunter that even though his question seems to be one poorly conceived, it requires a timely and in depth response so that the questioner will have absolutely no excuse to fall back on when he has demonstrated to the outfitter that he couldn't bag his game in a phone booth!

Now, for those of you who are novice hunters, here a few tips, not to be taken lightly.

1.) Do your homework. Read up on the animal you will be hunting.

2.) Don't expect that your guide will know things like where the animal will come from or when he will show up. Wild animals act and react in their own good time.

3.) Learn to be safe in the woods. You should carry survival gear, a compass you know how to read and even a GPS unit. Two watt radios can prove invaluable as well.

4.) Enjoy the hunt as a great experience of life. Laugh along with your guide when you screw up just as you laugh at him when he does something foolish. Hunting is meant to be enjoyed and if you are fortunate enough to harvest your animal, remember that this is just the icing on an otherwise enjoyable cake.

About the Author

Ray Dillon is well-known throughout New Brunswick, Canada and much of the New England states as an outfitter and outdoor writer. Born and raised on a small farm in the rural community of Zealand, he learned to hunt and fish with his Dad at an early age. His love of the woods and all that inhabits them and his enthusiasm for sharing the outdoor experience led him to start freelance writing for various Maritime, Canadian and US outdoor magazine publications and newspapers over twenty years ago. He is an active member of the Outdoor Writers Association of America and the New England Outdoor Writers Association and has co-authored four books about hunting/fishing. This book, a humorous anthology of sometimes unbelievable events that have actually transpired at his lodge, is his first solo book effort. Both the published book contributions and his regular monthly magazine articles have received very positive response from the outdoor fraternity! His love for the great outdoors influenced his decision to start an outdoor consumer's product field-testing company, "Dillon Outdoor Communications" and the outfitting business called "Malarkey Cabin Guiding Service" which has been going strong for the past fifteen years. Guiding hunters and fishers from the Continental United States and Europe has given him great pleasure over the years and innumerable campfire tales to share with outdoor enthusiasts. Mr. Dillon is a former member of the New Brunswick Wildlife Council, and a current member of the St. Anne-Nackawic and J.D Irving Woodlands advisory boards, the New Brunswick Alliance of Professional Outfitters Inc., Fredericton Fish and Game Association and New Brunswick Wildlife Federation. He resides with his wife Doreen at Keswick Ridge, New Brunswick.

About the Illustrator

Chas Goguen is a cartoonist born and raised in Saint John, New Brunswick. Being a cartoon, comic book and video game junkie throughout his youth, fueled the creative passion he possesses today. Through his artwork and storytelling, he loves to entertain others and make them laugh. His pride and joy is his self-produced comic book series entitled "Dotman", which spawned from a simple doodle in his elementary school workbook. "Dotman" can be viewed online at www.dotman.ca.